NEEDS-BASED EVANGELISM

". . . a fresh examination of what Christ has called the church to be."

–Rhymes H. Moncure Jr., Bishop, North Texas Annual Conference
of The United Methodist Church

". . . will help breathe new life into many mainline congregations."

–Kent Millard, Senior Pastor, St. Luke's United Methodist Church, Indianapolis,
Indiana

". . . a methodology for mobilizing the church's energy and commitment."

–Karen A. Greenwaldt, General Secretary,
The General Board of Discipleship, The United Methodist Church

---

"Tired of slick, Madison Avenue approaches that make 'evangelism' a dirty
word? *Needs-Based Evangelism* is for you!"

–Charles Crutchfield, Bishop, Arkansas Annual Conference
of The United Methodist Church

". . . profound and far reaching . . . "

–Frank Trotter, Senior Minister,
Metropolitan Memorial United Methodist Church, Washington, D.C.

". . . should be in every pastor's library and in the hands of laity who are asking
how the church can be renewed."

–William B. Oden, Retired Bishop of The United Methodist Church

NEEDS-BASED EVANGELISM

Being a Good Samaritan Church

ROBERT D. PIERSON

Abingdon Press
Nashville

NEEDS-BASED EVANGELISM
BEING A GOOD SAMARITAN CHURCH

Library of Congress Cataloging-in-Publication Data

Pierson, Robert D., 1936-
    Needs-based evangelism : being a good Samaritan church / Robert D. Pierson.
        p. cm.
    ISBN 0-687-33248-6 (binding: adhesive, pbk.)
    1. Evangelistic work. 2. Church growth. 3. Caring—Religious aspects—Christianity.
    I. Title.

    BV3790.P53 2006
    269'.2—dc22

2005033627

06 07 08 09 10 11 12 13 14 15—10 9 8 7 6 5 4 3 2 1

MANUFACTURED IN THE UNITED STATES OF AMERICA

CONTENTS

ACKNOWLEDGMENTS

The inspiration and information for this book comes, first, from the beautiful collegial relationship that I've had with the laity of Christ United Methodist Church in Tulsa, Oklahoma. Their partnership with me in ministry has been empowering. It has been Christ Church that has been the laboratory for developing the "Good Samaritan Church" and "Needs-Based Evangelism."

My inspiration has also come from my friends, associates, and acquaintances in ministry who have found the means and methodologies to become successful in reaching new people for Christ in a very secular world. These pastors of large and small churches across our nation are the real stories that prove that "needs-based evangelism" really does work. The primary inspiration for the book is the clear teachings of Jesus Christ, experienced daily in my ministry.

My encouragement has been my wife, Delia, our six children, my mother, and the staff and lay officers of Christ Church, who have all been so helpful and supportive. I particularly appreciate three persons who were so helpful in developing the idea and the manuscript: Harriett Olson and Kathy Armistead from Abingdon Press and Kristin Cole, a Christ Church support team member. I also greatly appreciate the other staff members of The United Methodist Publishing House and Christ United Methodist Church who have been so helpful in pulling together all the details of this manuscript.

I pray that these stories and concepts will provide both inspiration and instruction to the church that we love so much.

PREFACE

Today, there is crisis in mainline denominations. The great churches, such as the Methodist and Presbyterian and Episcopal churches, are experiencing a decline in growth. These denominations no longer are a part of the excitement of church growth and evangelistic outreach. Since 1969, The United Methodist Church has dropped from a membership of thirteen million to eight million at the beginning of the new millennium. This book is written out of a genuine concern for what is happening to the mainline Protestant church and to show how we can empower the local church to be strong and vital in new and effective ways. Today, the major phenomena that are affecting the mainline church are the rapid growth of independent charismatic fellowship or independent Bible fellowships, the general secularization of our society, the de-emphasis on faith and our heritage of faith, and the high level of commercialism. Pastors and lay members alike have lost their sense of excitement and vitality in the local church and have become passive in the midst of one of the greatest needs the world has ever experienced.

The purpose of this book is to provide a context of vitality and methodologies that work. For the past thirty years, I have been pastor of Christ United Methodist Church in Tulsa. When I went there, the church was struggling with less than two hundred in average attendance in the spring of 1969. By the year 2000, the attendance has grown to seventeen hundred. The church is in a declining neighborhood. It is an older facility, with limited parking, in a nongrowing part of the city, with limited local church funds. Despite these, in the last ten years, the church has moved from an average attendance of seven hundred to seventeen hundred.

I chair the Large Church Initiative of The United Methodist Church, and in that leadership for the last six years, I have been able to observe countless churches in difficult circumstances that are, nevertheless, growing with vitality, strength, and a deep sense of enthusiasm about leading people to Jesus Christ and building his kingdom.

I have also been a part of an organization called Churches United for Global Mission created by Dr. Robert Schuller as a fellowship of pastors of larger churches. It is out of my experience in a local church, and in a denominational and an ecumenical effort that I have written this book. My purpose is to bring the stories of churches and experienced pastors to bear on the essential question of how we rebuild mainline Protestant churches today.

DO OR DIE

Critical or Terminal

I sat in on one of the preliminary sessions of my denomination's international meetings. The speaker giving the laity address was articulate, enthusiastic, and well prepared. She punctuated her message by the proven technique of asking questions of the audience, hoping to engage our imaginations with hers. She said, "What will your church be like in twenty or thirty years?" The question sent me into a downward spiral of melancholy feeling about the great denomination that I had given my life to. My parents, grandparents, and great-grandparents, and as far as the obituaries in our family could record, had all been Methodists for 150 years. This General Conference speaker asked me, and all of us, where we would be in thirty years. To informed, logical, scientific-minded individuals, the answer was simple. We will be gone. Just look at the statistics. Check the trends. Read the facts. We are dying.

Car manufacturers change models and styles by looking at the trends. Major corporations change their sales by studying the trends. Management looking at the trends change products. Presidents and presidential candidates write their speeches and plan their campaigns based upon the trends. The trends tell most mainline Protestants that in thirty years, our denominations will be gone.

Most mainline Protestant denominations' members are over sixty years of age, and in thirty years, they will be gone from the planet. What I mean is that our denominations will be gone. Despite a few hopeful, enthusiastic signs of growth across the mainline Protestant denominations, trends indicate that we will simply vanish into statistical oblivion. The number of our new members is far less than our losses. Even attendance in worship, which is the best indication of health, is down and has been declining every year for several years.

In the midst of this general decline of mainline churches, disagreements over social and political issues continually pull us apart. Lutherans, Presbyterians, and Episcopalians have experienced schism after schism. Other denominations continue to divide and decline. Lyle Schaller, writing in the months before the 2004 General Conference of The United Methodist Church, clarified in his book *The Ice Cube Is Melting* what could happen. I was asked to read Lyle's manuscript about possible schism in my own denomination. I received a copy of it in December 2003. In the midst of the joy of Christmas, I was filled with depression because of what Lyle described could happen in my beloved church. Lyle has been my coach and friend for many years (as he has been for so many clergy), and to read his description of possible schism was very discouraging. What has happened to Presbyterians, Lutherans, Episcopalians, and others is happening to us. Because we cannot agree and diversity continues to pull us apart, we have lost our vitality; and our energy seems to be directed mostly toward disagreeing. But church and secular media report not on the strength and vitality of great denominations, but on our idiosyncrasies, our divisions, and our disagreements. The media often portrays us not as vibrant, helpful, enthusiastic, and growing, but as confused, angry, disappointed, and declining. This unbalanced reporting is disheartening.

The Church Bell Curve

To the dismal showing of mainline American Protestantism, the answer may be that we simply understand that God used us in the past, and now we are no longer effective. Are we used up, worn out, impractical to recycle, and irrelevant to the kingdom? It would make sense that God raised up these great denominations for a valid purpose. If that purpose still exists, and the potential is still there, and the people of faith are still faithful to fulfilling that purpose, then these churches are still needed.

In the analysis of social institutions that has been done by countless experts in organizational development, sociology, or institutional typology, the usual description of the life of an organization is the typical bell curve—slow growth at first, rapid growth, institutionalization, plateau, decline, rapid decline, slow inevitable death. But if something happens along the way, when the bell curve begins to turn down to change the decline, then growth happens again. If a similar phenomenon that started the movement happens again, the movement is revitalized. Businesses that were dying can take on new life. Marriages that seemed to be over can blossom again. Colleges that lived with dying sports programs can win their division.

Renewal and regeneration can happen, but always, always, in every institution, in every religious movement, certain things must be done. It is always true for all organizational life: you "do or die." A bookstore sells books or goes out of business. A professional singer entertains or does not work. An auto repair shop repairs cars or goes slowly out of business. A country provides vital answers and services for its citizens, or it becomes weak and dies, is absorbed, or is conquered. It always works that way. Churches are no different.

I believe we are called to change the direction of our downward curve. Our goal is not to deal with preventing death, but to focus on life, vigor, growth, and hope. Our goal is not just to study how the institution functions, but how the institution of the church functions following the way of Jesus Christ. Our goal is not denominational survival, but kingdom expansion. Our goal is not necessarily to fill a mega-church sanctuary. Our goal is to help people follow Jesus Christ so the world is made better. Our goal is not to create new denominational bureaucracies and denominational heroes. Our goal is to help people experience, believe, and live a life of faithfulness and fulfillment.

Measuring Success, Quality, and Quantity

In the free enterprise system, numbers evaluate everything. What was the profit? How much were the sales? What are the salaries? What are the dividends? Are things better or worse than last year? Sometimes this way of thinking seems very obnoxious to men and women of faith. Someone once told me that we were called to be not super salesmen, but faithful Christians. Though this statement sounded sweet, it is an illusion. Many mainline Protestant Christians today will decide to wrap themselves in a blanket of self-righteousness and cover their heads with a pillow saying, "Our goal is quality, not quantity! We do not want to be a part of the diluting of the gospel by emphasizing numbers." For at least fifty years, mainline Protestant Christians have often covered their ineffectiveness by saying that they were only interested in "quality."

We have been more concerned with following the liturgical year and preaching from the lectionary in the "correct" way than reaching people with the gospel. We have been more concerned with not getting too excited, staying very cognitive; and as a result, we are losing an entire generation of so-called post-moderns. Some of us have been angry with the excesses of various expressions of faith and have refused to raise our hands in worship for fear that some denominational executive would think we had gone charismatic; and in the meantime, we have lost half our congregations to the booming new churches that understand the need people have, not only for the cognitive, but also for the emotional. We have allowed the carnival-like services of television evangelists to provide the only hope for men and women who are hurting in the desperateness of modern life. We have been afraid to risk promising anything other than a comfortable pew to those who have lost their jobs, who are crippled with arthritis, who are dying with cancer, or who are depressed over children lost to drugs. Too often, the only practical answer that most of those people can find is the television evangelists' circus; the excitement of reality TV; addictions to sex, work, or alcohol; upward mobility; or another visit to the family doctor.

Too often, we mainline Protestant churches have simply not been involved, not meeting the needs of these people and sometimes not even willing to risk giving them a little bit of hope. Certainly, quality is important, but the concern needs to be the quality of real ministry to the needs of people, not concerned about some irrelevant point of view or some escapism theology or denominational bureaucracy or a commitment to an irrelevant theological position. Most assuredly, the questions that need to be asked about quality are about meeting real needs: *Does worship provide a real experience of the presence of God? Is the sacrament presented in such a quality way that hope and understanding of the risen Christ is actually experienced? Are our education programs for children, youth, and adults dealing with the biblical material in a way that is relevant to the issues facing individuals and families?* The question is effectiveness.

Within all the denominational groups that are showing decline, there are examples of the reverse. There are churches that are growing, that have excitement and vitality in every kind of neighborhood and cultural situation. But overall, the culture of these churches is radically different from the so-called mainline Protestant churches. The growing church is entrepreneurial, biblical, charismatic, and experiential. The effective church does worship well, is socially sensitive, and is meeting the needs of every age group. The problem is that so many churches in America have not experienced revitalization, redevelopment, reimaging, or reinventing. They are justifying their failures by blaming denominational structures, entrepreneurial methods of other churches, and the perpetual problem of laity and clergy working together.

Consumerism or the Attack of the Shoppers

In the midst of this kind of decline and division, we are in a culture of extreme consumerism. The prosperity following the Second World War has led us to a compulsive desire to have what we want. We have become consumers driven by culture. We want the best at the best price. Old ideas of loyalty that held churches together and made denominations strong are simply nonexistent. Today's goal is shopping. We want to find the best for our money, and, consequently, mainline churches are scrambling to compete with new entrepreneurial, independent Bible and independent charismatic fellowships. The truth is that mainline churches are losing dramatically. Christians in the United States today demand the right to choose and the freedom to attend whatever church is most attractive. Potential new Christians are attracted to churches that offer worship, preaching, ministries, and programs that meet their needs.

A young dad came into my office. Troy had grown up in our church. He explained that he and his family decided to attend a new charismatic mega-church in town. I was bewildered at his seemingly logical, calm approach to the decision. He said he loved his home church. He and his wife had learned much and had been led spiritually from being a part of our church, but he wanted the best he could get for his children. Troy explained that the children's program at the large charismatic fellowship was the best in town. It had new facilities, use of drama, media, and all the "bells and whistles" that money could buy. He went on to explain that their priority was their children and that they were going to the church that had the best children's program in town.

I explained that we were developing a new children's program, and we needed his help. We were seeking to have the finest program we could. We talked about the importance of the beliefs of his family. But Troy and his wife had already made the decision. They had enrolled their kids in the other Sunday school the previous week.

Today, in most mainline Protestant churches, families are making similar decisions. Most pastors of mainline churches could tell the story over and over. Loyalty is second. Shopping is first. Our culture wants choice and wants the best. Loyalty to denominational beliefs, theological perspective, tradition, and family simply is not important. We shop for cars today to find the best deal. When my father was raising our family in a small rural community in Oklahoma, Dad always drove Plymouth or Dodge cars. He was a Chrysler products man. There was in the culture of the average American loyalty to products and companies. Today we buy a car that offers the best deal, the best price, and the best warranty. Product loyalty is not there. Brand loyalty is simply gone.

For the mainline churches to reach out to new people and to grow, we must understand that we are competing in a consumer-driven society. The old rules are changed.

4

Loyalty is gone. Choice is good. People attend churches where they can get the services they want and, most important, they will attend a church where their needs are met.

The Post-Christian Era

Consumerism is not just expressed in terms of competition with new Bible fellowships and mega-churches. The competition is, basically, with the very secular world. Sociologists describe American society today as post-Christian, meaning that sometime in the last twenty or thirty years, the majority of Christian influence has been lost. Our society is dominated by a much more secular attitude. This struggle is not just an issue about whether or not we allow the "under God" to be in the Pledge of Allegiance or the Ten Commandments to be in public buildings. It is a very secular world we live in today. Somewhere back in the 1990s, the church lost its dominance in American culture. With the compulsion to have the freedom to choose whatever we want, we have decided that choice is our real god. Consequently, the great heritage of faith that was so much a part of American and other national cultures is no longer present, and our god is freedom. By being predominantly a secular society, we have lost the influence of values, of faith, the message of Jesus Christ, a focus on prayer, the strength of the local church, and the authority of clergy. The spokespersons for our culture are the entertainment idols. The places of community are the clubs and bars, Little League baseball games, school and community activities, professional sports events, concerts, movies, and other media events. The court ruling of no prayer at football games is simply a way of telling the church, "you are no longer in control." The struggle is a cultural struggle in which the influence of the church has lessened significantly.

Sally, the mom of a teenager, stands at the door of the church on Sunday morning and tells her pastor that their family will not be back at church until soccer season is over because the soccer games are being played on Sunday mornings. Sally sees no problem in what she told the pastor; simply her family will be gone because soccer is a priority. Church once lived in a culture in which Sunday and Wednesday evening were church times. We no longer live in that kind of culture. We are competing with secular ideas that replace traditional values of the church in competition with the new consumer-driven, often self-centered society.

Often, secularism also creates a negative attitude toward the church. Criticism of right-wing fundamentalism and socially involved liberals has become common conversation in the media and modern culture. Churches all across the United States are seeking to raise the money to purchase property and relocate, but they find that the local community is very much opposed to a church being placed in their neighborhood. Where developers once reserved sites for churches, now those developers are opposing churches being placed in their developments. Things have changed. The attitude of the government and the public is not always favorable to the development of the church.

Time to Decide to Grow

Recently, I visited two churches in the downtown area of a major American metropolitan area. The churches were right across the street from each other, both with similar facilities, theology, and denominational structure. One was booming, flourishing, and seeking to build or to add a satellite. The other was voting to close. The obvious question is: "What made the difference?" These are the kinds of choices facing today's American church.

The baby boomers created a culture of shoppers, without brand loyalty. Certainly, this methodology creates better prices and better products, but for so many churches, it creates only growing failure. Secularism of our society is pervasive. The ineffectiveness of the church today to compete with this secular society has created the image of a church that is irrelevant, and too often one that people see as foolish. But this ideological, experiential, amoral, secular, consumer-driven society is the world in which God has called us to make disciples of Jesus Christ.

The pioneer method of church development and church growth, set by American pioneers moving west, was to do what was necessary to get churches started in new communities. These pioneer American preachers and laity did what was necessary to create Christian community, meet needs, set a tone of morality, and provide leadership for the emerging towns and cities across America. Those techniques from frontier America simply have been forgotten. We have lost our ability to innovate, create, and compete.

Even more tragic is that, too often, we have lost the energy, the concern, and the passion. Many American clergy are concerned more about retirement, benefits, security, and getting out of the ministry. The passion is gone. Too often, clergy and lay leaders alike are not even concerned about the proliferation of an immoral culture, the growing numbers of persons of all ages who do not know Christ, the lack of Christlike social justice and care, and the decline of the church. Much of the American church seems paralyzed to stand, to influence, to change, or to evangelize.

In this situation, God is calling us to break our addictions to mediocrity and complacency to become evangelists! Needs-based evangelism is what Jesus modeled with his life. Growing churches are churches meeting needs. They are "good Samaritan" churches, stopping to help. They are bringing Christ to people through positive, compassionate love.

In our highly secular, consumer-driven society, it is time for the Christian to decide really to follow Christ. In a culture and society that is continually changing by the rapid development of technology, it is time for the Christian to stand as the author of truth. Jesus always asked people to decide to let their light shine, to forgive their enemies, to become fishers of people, to take up their cross, and to make a difference. Today, Jesus is asking Christians to decide again. The decisions today are no different than they were in the first century. They have to do with values, time, energy, risk, commitment, and meeting needs. As always, if we will decide, God's victory will be ours.

In many churches all across America, laity and clergy have decided that making disciples of Jesus Christ is the priority, and growth is happening! They have decided to meet needs, to do what Jesus taught! We will proclaim God's amazing grace. We will be like the good Samaritan and meet needs. It is because leaders make such decisions that things will be different, we will compete, and we will reach the secular world. We must decide to care, decide to notice, decide to help, decide to innovate, decide to disciple, decide to strategize, decide to market, decide to pray, decide to worship, decide to compete, decide to prune, decide to toughen, decide to evangelize, and decide to revolutionize. Because decision-making is so complicated, we simply put it off; we procrastinate. We are, too often, the Christian procrastinators—secular, weak, and afraid—so we decide not to decide. We hang in the ambiguity of being comfortable as pastors and lay leaders and simply "go with the flow." Whatever the culture says, it must be right. If it is on the evening news or the talk show host says it's so, it must be true. We just go with the flow and never decide. Because of this, we are losing opportunity after opportunity.

Now is the time to change. We must decide to reach our community with the good news of Christ. The message of the church is one that meets the basic needs of all. We are called to decide to notice the hurts and brokenness and to respond with love and help. Laity and clergy in churches across America need to join in a covenant to reach new people for Christ, to make strong disciples, and to make sure that every new person we win to Christ becomes not only a disciple, but also a missionary and an evangelist.

Several years ago, I visited a church in Pelsin, Czechoslovakia. It is one of the strongest churches in Europe. Despite communism, persecution, and the loss of their church property during the political turmoil, they were growing in fantastic ways, spiritually and numerically. How was such growth possible? The simple story the church leaders told me was that there were three "elderly ladies" who, after their church building had been taken from them and made into a communist propaganda hall, met regularly in one of their apartments to pray that God would help them take back their church and lead people to Jesus. They met and prayed for three years, and their prayers were answered. Many people of Pelsin found out about the three old ladies who were praying, and they joined them. Eventually, a pastor was appointed to lead this growing group of Methodist Christians in Pelsin. They decided that they needed to take back their church building. On Saturday evening each week, they would march around the church building time and time again, praying that God would help them get back the church building. Their numbers grew and grew, and people were baptized and committed to Christ. Eventually, the key secular leader of the city, himself, was led to Jesus. He influenced the government to give back the church to the United Methodists in the center of Pelsin. Hundreds were led to Jesus Christ as a result.

A United Methodist church in Ft. Lauderdale, Florida, was influenced by the small group prayer movement from South Africa. Its pastor, Dick Wills, saw a means by which new people could be led to Jesus through the small group movement, and a program of recovery ministry was developed. Needs were met. The church became strong and vital—one of the strongest in the denomination— simply because they decided to respond to needs. A Lutheran pastor in Phoenix, along with the laity of his church, decided that they would do something new and relevant to meet the needs of younger people. Contemporary worship was born in a new way. Walt Kallestad, of the Lutheran

Church of Joy, set an example of growth that has developed a large complex of facilities to meet needs. Their model has become an example to change church after church in many denominations.

Bill Hybels and a group of young friends made the decision to make a difference, and the church that was to become Willow Creek Community Church in Chicago started in a movie theatre with a group of kids. They now are one of the largest churches in America. Hybels and the Willow Creek team of leaders made their church a major training place for churches to learn more relevant and needs-based worship, ministry, and programming. Dr. John Vaughan's research on the fastest-growing churches in the United States indicates that, before 1970, there were only ten churches with an attendance of more than two thousand. Today there are more than one thousand churches of that size.

They did it. All of us can do it. We just have to decide to do it.

A Call

These are stories of laity and clergy partnering to make a difference. They are not necessarily stories of miraculous leaders or wealthy, powerful people. They are stories of ordinary Christians who decided to make a difference. We must decide to do whatever is necessary to lead people to Jesus Christ. In 1 Corinthians 9:19-23, Paul challenged Christians to do whatever is necessary. Unless we do this today, we shall die!

Paul made it so radically clear in these words at the end of 1 Corinthians 9. He spoke about becoming "all things to all people, that I might by all means save some." That radical statement of being willing to do whatever is necessary to lead people to Christ is desperately needed by ordinary Christians today. We have not evaluated our behavior as Christians reaching out to new people. Paul's unusual statement calls us to do what we must do to reach new people for Jesus Christ. The example that Paul, Jesus, and the other writers used is to do the most loving thing—to help, to love, and to care. Today, we must decide if we are willing to do acts of kindness and love, to make an invitation, and to lead people to become followers of Jesus Christ.

The following chapters outline a methodology and a means for mobilizing the church's energy for doing what is authentic, needed, and effective in helping the world find the wonderful power of God through Jesus Christ.

In 2005, Schaller wrote *A Mainline Turnaround* (Nashville: Abingdon Press), describing detailed strategies for changing the mainline church decline. In this book, he outlines a multitude of proven and effective strategies that can work to turn mainline churches around. The concept of needs-based evangelism provides particular strategies that are compatible with mainline church theology and is already a part of mainline churches' self-understanding and basic programming. Needs-based evangelism is biblically sound, proven in effectiveness, and natural for the church and the individual Christian to do.

CHAPTER 2

NEEDS-BASED EVANGELISM: AN ANCIENT ANSWER FOR A REAL FUTURE

The Mission Statement for the Jesus Church

Jesus walked into his hometown church. When it came time for the Scripture read-ing and the leader invited anyone to read, Jesus stood, took the Bible, and read from Isaiah, "The Spirit of the Lord is upon me, because he has anointed me to bring good news to the poor. He has sent me to proclaim release to the captives and recovery of sight to the blind, to let the oppressed go free, to proclaim the year of the Lord's favor" (Luke 4:18-19). Those words spoken by Jesus have become the simple outline for ser-mons and Sunday school lessons over the years, and behind them is a basic message. Jesus said he came to meet our needs. The litany of things he described in his coming was simply a litany of human needs. In that simple statement said in Nazareth a long time ago, Jesus outlined one of the most effective means of leading new people to find the power of God in their lives—that is, to show them how God's love meets their needs. His mission statement can be our church's mission statement, "We have been called to meet needs."

In Luke 10:25-37, Jesus is in a discussion about what is really necessary to go to heaven or to find life. The conclusion of the argument is simple: "Love God and love your neighbor as yourself." Jesus said to do that and you will really live. But it seemed hard to understand. So he told a story about what it would look like. We call it the story of the "good Samaritan." As he concluded that story, Jesus said to go and do the same thing. It is the only story that Jesus told in which he concluded by saying we were to do that very same thing. It is the story of a Samaritan simply responding to a need.

In Matthew 25:31-46, Jesus describes judgment day and separating the sheep from the goats. He tells us that the sheep are those who help others. They will go to be with God; those that do not help are out. Then he explains a very powerful concept that is key to bringing people into a relationship with him: When we help someone in need, he is present.

Preachers, pastors, theologians, apostles, bishops, and ordinary Christians search for what it means to lead people to Christ, and we have devised many ways to do it. We hold revival meetings, camp meetings, and prayer meetings. We have pipe organs, praise bands, guitars, harps, flutes, and anything else we can think of, to lead in our worship. Some of us raise our hands, and some bow our heads. Some shout and yell, and others are utterly quiet. We search for ways to witness. We stand on street corners and yell at passersby. We send multicolored postcards with clever graphics. We knock on doors, make telephone calls, send out personal letters, and employ countless other means to try to reach new people for Jesus Christ.

The last thing that Jesus said before he ascended into heaven was to go into all the world and preach the gospel (Matthew 28:19-20). We are called to teach what Jesus taught. We are called to make disciples. On the day of Pentecost, the followers of Jesus modeled for us what we are called to do: lead people to become followers of Jesus and become a part of his church. Yet we continue to struggle with how to do it. In the history of Christianity, there is one approach that always works, and that is the approach Jesus began with: meet the needs of the people and proclaim the gospel.

The Good Samaritan Model

In the story of the good Samaritan, Jesus was in the midst of an argument with a lawyer. The challenge was what you have to do get to heaven, to be okay with God. Jesus' answer as found in Matthew 22 and Luke 10 was simple. We call them the Great Commandments—love God, and love your neighbor as yourself. But the lawyer was not satisfied with that answer. Like many people, he wanted to know more. *So who is my neighbor?* the lawyer asked To answer this, Jesus told one of the most powerful, simple, clear stories in the Bible—the story of the good Samaritan, the story of meeting needs.

Strategies for growth in the mainline church today can include mass evangelism, confrontational witnessing, extensive advertising programs, new elaborate facilities, high-tech worship, and media-enhanced preaching. *But, unless needs are met, growth won't happen.* My church, The United Methodist Church, has for its entire existence focused on meeting needs. John Wesley's preaching in the fields or at the factories was to meet needs. The circuit riders moving across America, bringing the gospel, sought to meet needs. Whether by creating institutions of higher education in America or organizing homes for children, retired people, the homeless, and the marginalized, we know how to meet needs.

My denomination, along with many other mainline denominations, has been institutionally specialized in helping with the social issues of our community; where there is hurt or brokenness, we have been there to help. We know how to meet needs.

What Is Needs-Based Evangelism?

We must combine clearly and enthusiastically our ability to meet needs with a proclamation of the gospel. If all we do is meet needs, we do not point people to the One who empowers us to meet those needs; instead, we witness only to ourselves. Making this connection between meeting needs and proclaiming the gospel should be as automatic as a tissue is to a sneeze, as a bandage is to a cut, as a hug is to tears.

A new program of evangelism needs to be instituted intensely all across the church. We must combine a caring ministry with proclamation of the gospel. We must witness as we share and help. When the homeless are fed, they need to be invited to our churches. When the youth are on a church basketball team, it should include prayer and worship. When a parenting class is offered, the gospel needs to be proclaimed. This is needs-based evangelism.

The leadership of the church needs to be committed to developing needs-based evangelism programs across the church. Wherever the needs are, the church should be there with the gospel of Jesus Christ, leading people to a better way of life. In the past, we have developed too many programs and activities within our churches that are nothing more than busy work to help us feel better about being in church. All of our programs need to be focused evangelistic ministry—ministry that includes the sharing of the gospel. With every program possibility considered, the leadership of local churches should ask, *Will this lead people to find and follow Christ?* It may be fun, fascinating, interesting, and entertaining, but unless it helps people find and follow Christ, it should never be a priority.

A congregation was discussing the possibility of a community drug rehabilitation program at their church. The need was obvious. The program they were considering was government-funded. Mary, the mother of a son who had serious drug problems, led the group advocating the program. In the midst of the discussion, Kevin, a thirty-five-year-old new church member, changed the direction of the plan. He explained that he had been a drug user for years and was now clean. He agreed with the need, and he felt the church should start a faith-based rehabilitation program where good therapy and good faith were presented *together*. Today that church has over one hundred people each week at the Friday evening recovery program and worship. Most of the one hundred are now involved in all the church life.

Built on Grace

Needs-based evangelism is one of the most effective and clear means of reaching new people for Jesus Christ. Churches all across America that are clearly meeting the needs of the people in the community are growing. When we combine the authentic social gospel with authentic evangelistic witness, people are led to Christ. This concept is like a two-edged sword. It must have both edges to work: real compassion, care, and help, coupled with authentic witness and sharing of the gospel. It need not be obnoxious, arrogant, or manipulative. It is simply sharing the loving truth.

Robert Schuller founded one of the largest and most influential churches in America, the Crystal Cathedral in Garden Grove, California, in a drive-in theater. For many years, he held the Institute for Church Leadership. And in his Institute, he would describe their strategy of evangelism. He described it simply as, "Find a need, and meet it." That idea is both biblical and effective.

Windsor Village United Methodist Church in Houston is the largest church in the United Methodist denomination. When Kirbyjon Caldwell began his ministry at Windsor Village, he combined powerful evangelistic preaching and a practical understanding of the needs of people. Today, Windsor Village provides a fascinating combination of exciting worship and relevant ministry. A former shopping center has been converted into a center providing help for the community.

Needs-based evangelism is built first upon grace. In most evangelists' favorite scripture, John 3:16-17, we read, "For God so loved the world that he gave his only Son, so that everyone who believes in him may not perish but may have eternal life. Indeed, God did not send the Son into the world to condemn the world, but in order that the world might be saved through him." Perhaps the most important part in that scripture to understand is that Christ came not to condemn the world. The basis of the relationship with God through Jesus Christ is love. It is amazing grace. For needs-based evangelism to work, it must begin with authentic, non-manipulative care. It is genuine acceptance.

A nine-year-old boy invites his friend to Sunday school, not because he gets a prize from the teacher, but because he cares about his friend and wants to share something precious. A teenager brings her friend to the youth program because she cares. A sixty-eight-year-old woman who invites her friend to the choir concert at Christmas does it because she cares and wants her friend to enjoy the music. Effective evangelism happens when a church seeks to help families in crisis, marriages in difficulty, lonely people find wholeness, depressed adolescents find solutions, broken-hearted lovers rebuild their relationships. The invitation to Christ and his church becomes a part of the experience of his love.

Meeting Needs and Ministry

The examples of caring congregations are found all across the church. Over and over, real ministry means growth. Churches across America have adopted recovery programs during which a Friday night worship service focuses on the powerful keys of the Twelve-Step Program, and church leaders are there, open to care and love. People are led not only to a methodology of recovery, but also to Christ and to become participants in the way of Jesus.

Youth programs with vital, relevant teachings to help kids deal with radically troubling aspects of our society help adolescents find ways not only to cope, survive, and succeed, but also to find Jesus.

Among the most basic needs facing any American today is, how to get along with people? This what a Christian understands clearly: to know that God loves us first and that Jesus taught us how to live.

We seem to be afraid to deal directly with real human needs. We become captured by old stereotypes, styles of ministry, and irrelevant cliques. We often get caught in a complicated network of solving problems that don't exist and offer cures to issues that are not there. The reason we fail in our ability to reach new people for Christ is that we are irrelevant.

Walk through the personal growth section of your bookstore. There are volumes and volumes of books about how to get along together. In the love chapter, 1 Corinthians 13, four verses provide seven things to do and seven things not to do that can remedy most human relationship problems. Needs-based evangelism is delivering the basic message of the gospel of Jesus Christ, which Paul says in Romans 13:8 is love. The teachings of the New Testament are the best self-helps ever written on successful relationships.

A small, rural Oklahoma church began focusing their energy on meeting the needs of children in the community. With their weekday after-school program, they had more kids and adults in church for their expanded Wednesday night kids' witness program than they did on Sunday morning. For small and large churches, needs-based kids programs work and often reach the whole family.

Growing churches have programs and ministries to help families function—marriages become healthy, and personal communication becomes more effective. Workshops, retreats, training, and counseling can heal, help, and bring people to a church. The church of Christ is a community of love, learning, and healing.

One of the major areas of broken relationships today is divorce. Fifty percent of American marriages end in divorce. Mainline Protestant churches that believe in the grace of our Lord, Jesus Christ, should be leading the country in the ministry of helping people get through divorce. However, the opposite seems to be true. Mainline churches run from the issue of divorce. We run from the opportunity to help. Those few that help seem to help in a way that, instead of building up the person who has gone through this devastating experience, makes him or her feel guiltier. People make decisions for Christ when they have gone through difficult transitions. There is no more difficult transition in American life than going through divorce. The church needs to be there with all of its wisdom and power, loving help, and generosity.

The church I pastor has a strong divorce ministry built out of the context of an aggressive and caring singles program. We find that if forty people attend the Divorce Adjustment Workshop, thirty of those people will make a new or first-time commitment to Christ and twenty of them will become active in our church.

When needs are met, decisions are made.

Two members of our congregation were on a short vacation and attended a small rural church across the state in Oklahoma. It was an informal service. The pastor asked visitors to stand and introduce themselves. Gerald and Nancy were the only visitors there that Sunday, and so it was obvious who they were as they stood and introduced themselves and said a word about the church they came from in Tulsa. When the service was over, a lady rushed up to them and said she had been to their church. She had gone through the Divorce Adjustment Workshop, and then she said what so many have said, "It saved my life."

Meeting needs can mean the saving of life not only physically, but also spiritually. We must commit ourselves to a total ministry of helping people through their difficulties in life and, consequently, bringing them to the throne of God through Jesus Christ.

Needs-Based Evangelism Is Strategic

Needs-based evangelism is simply strategic. People make decisions when they go through a crisis. When everything is going well, most of us don't want to change. Why would we change our ways, accept Christ, become a new person, and make decisions for a moral and accountable life when everything is going great? But when our marriage comes apart, or we lose our job, or a chemical imbalance in our brain makes us deeply depressed, or a teenager is arrested for use of drugs, then we are open to deal with life in a new way, to hear the truth of God's wonderful love, and to make the decision to accept Jesus as the answer.

The cultural prosperity of today lets us think that everything is fine. In the midst of the crisis of relationships, when polarity within our nation is high, in a world where we talk about the problems of drug abuse, degeneration of marriage, sexual abuse, and child abuse, we still convey to one another that everything is fine. Yet a millimeter below the surface, it is not fine at all.

Needs-based evangelism is built on an understanding that we are called to be a good Samaritan church; to respond to the needs; to see beneath the surface of superficial prosperity where the hurt is; to understand that we are called, as best we can, to bring the power of the gospel of Jesus Christ to meet those needs. When the church helps, that happens. People find not only the healing results of the love of Christ, but also Christ, himself, in their lives.

The old idea that we can divide the Christian faith into two tasks—evangelism and social concerns—is as ridiculous theologically and not helpful for the church as any of the heresies the church has allowed over the years. They are the same.

The description of Christ's own ministry that is found in Luke 4 is the description of caring, of bringing good news to the entire human situation.

The methodology for needs-based evangelism is basic Christianity. First, it begins with a commitment to follow Jesus, follow what he taught and what he said. Second, it involves a willingness to help, to meet the needs of others. Third, we must be open to what those needs are and see where we, as individuals and as churches, have resources to help. God does not expect us to solve every issue, but to solve some. The local church can provide some solutions. Most of the time, solutions don't need to be complicated. For most of the needs that people have today, the most powerful help is simply love. The amazing grace that Jesus has given us opens us not only to be able to help, but also to be able to love, and it becomes the means of reaching others for Christ. Nonjudgmental needs-meeting is one of the most powerful means of opening the door between an individual and Jesus Christ.

Our acts of kindness and love should be done in the most professional, caring, effective ways we know, trusting that God will use our efforts like seeds planted to bring fruit. In all aspects of our meeting needs, the gospel needs to be presented. Too often, Christians help but do not explain why they help. Too often, Christians want to do noninvolved caring. Therefore, we never have the opportunity to explain about the God who loves us despite our sins. Real needs-based evangelism must involve clear, gentle witnessing. It needs to be cradled in the arms of the local church. Evangelism is ineffective when it is done as an impersonal social service in the community. It is ineffective when it is done at arms length. Evangelism works when it involves people one-on-one, up close, helping.

The Local Church Is the Basic Evangelism Unit

The local church is the home base of our caring. The church family is the experience of love: our love and God's love! Jesus is seen in us. Jesus is understood when we explain why we are there, why we are helping. People come to follow Christ when they see an example and hear your story and the explanation for helping. As people are helped through the ministries of a local church, they become involved in the church. Needs-based evangelism is best done by individual churches, not as churches working in ecumenical teams. People who are being helped need to identify with the local church community that is helping. If not, they will see Christ, experience the power of grace, and not have family to relate to, to be nurtured and helped and encouraged through. That is why needs-based evangelism is basically a local church plan. It is not organized by conferences, districts, and judicatories. It is done by congregations so that the amazing grace that is shared in helping is identified with a community of loving followers of Jesus. In this way, the person receiving the experience of Christ knows where to find the growth, support, and long-term affirmation. The local church is the basic evangelism unit.

CHAPTER 3

THE POWER OF BELIEF

What We Believe Is Key

He sat across my office, a forty-two-year-old clergyman, articulate, intelligent, and well-educated. The words he spoke were simple: "I'm a failure. I don't know what to do. It's not satisfying anymore. I feel like I am losing. I want to be a good pastor. I don't know what to do." He vented, we talked, I listened.

What he said represented the feelings of so many pastors of mainline Protestant churches. Our commitment is strong, our education is the best available, our churches once were the center of the communities in both small and large towns, but now things are not working so well. Attendance is down, membership is declining, and congregations are restless. We believe we are doing the right things, the sermons are prepared, the music is good, and the curriculum from our denomination is excellent. It is just that there are few new people. Most of the time, attendance is declining. How can we turn it around? Where do we begin?

Our beliefs are the key. What we believe in and are committed to make the real difference. One of the theories of human motivation and behavior suggests that the beginning of behavior is belief. It is conviction that starts the process of behavioral change, creative ideas, and new behavior. Our basic beliefs influence our attitudes, and our attitudes direct our behavior.

The Great Commission

At the time of his ascension, Jesus gave us what we call the Great Commission—to go into the entire world, to preach and teach, to spread the good news (Matthew 28:18-20). The first action of the early church, as described in Acts 2, is reaching out to new people for Christ. Paul says in 1 Corinthians 9 that we should do whatever is necessary in order to make disciples of Christ. These three scriptures represent the imperative for a Christian. Jesus instructs us to go into all the world. He instructs us to teach, to make disciples. Here, clearly, in the understanding of the early church, as well as in the understanding of Christ's clear instructions, we are called to be evangelists. Pastors and laity can find themselves occupied with the busy work of church life, with tasks such as organizing potluck dinners, redecorating the church parlor, seeing that the toilets are properly cleaned, and planting daffodils in flowerbeds. We can be busy. Yet, unless we fulfill the Great Commission of making disciples, our beliefs are hypocritical and we are busy doing things that don't matter.

The first description of the followers of Jesus in the book of Acts is people leading others to Jesus Christ. The preaching of Peter and the others was preaching that called people to make a commitment and become a part of the church. The second chapter of Acts ends with a description of the activity and life of the church and the numbers of persons who had become members. To respond to the biblical message, Christians must respond to the imperative to be evangelists. There are many things to do as a church, but unless we do the basics, we do not grow. We do not have the people to do the things that bring justice, peace, and kindness to the world. Unless we have the power of a healthy institution made up of a multiplicity of persons, we simply cannot accomplish any good biblical task.

Paul, writing in 1 Corinthians 9, explains simply that he would do anything to lead someone to Jesus Christ. This passage gives us an understanding of the priority of the work of evangelism. Needs-based evangelism calls us not to do inauthentic methodologies in leading persons to Christ, but to do what Jesus taught, caring and loving and sharing the gospel. Too many times in the enthusiasm to follow the Great Commission, Christians have been willing to manipulate, scare, and mislead people in order to add more to the church. Our methodology in doing what is necessary is still the authentic message of Jesus Christ. Meeting needs to reach people for Christ is authentic.

For the mainline Protestant church of today to grow, for needs-based evangelism to work, we must make a cognitive decision based upon our beliefs. We must decide that the purpose of the church is to make disciples, that our task as clergy is to be evangelistic, and that every program and activity of a local church needs to be evaluated on its effectiveness in reaching new people for Christ. It is time for all of us to call one another to accountability, an accountability of belief. Do you believe that the message of Jesus Christ is the will of God? Do you believe that the church of Jesus Christ was created by God to do God's good work? Do you believe that our task is to help people find and follow Jesus Christ? Do you believe that our purpose is to make disciples? Do you believe that we are called to be the church? Do you believe that both laity and clergy are needed to be evangelists, to be instrumental in the same thing that happened on the day of Pentecost? Do you believe our task is to join God in the building of the church, the leading of people to Christ, meeting human needs, the task of building a just world? Do you believe the Great Commission?

Answering *yes* to this series of commitment questions is the healthy basis of church growth and evangelism. Unless the clergy and key laity of a congregation believe, then evangelism is nothing more than some panic, survival mentality saying that we must grow or we can't pay the bills; or it is some arrogant form of jealousy that if the new Bible churches can grow, we can grow too. Those reasons for growth are simply superficial and will be swept away with the changing seasons. We must begin the evangelism task with an inner commitment to win people for Jesus Christ because we believe that is right. This is the Great Commission.

New Missionaries in a Foreign Land

The highly secular world of the twenty-first century creates for the Christian an environment that is often hostile. The culture can be offensive, the morality nonexistent, and the compassion manipulative. This secular world is often hostile to loving, kindness, true justice, personal integrity, and, most of all, the simple message of Jesus Christ. We are called to be like new missionaries in a foreign land. We are serving God in a culture that is foreign to our values, customs, and beliefs, seeking to lead people to become a part of our fellowship of caring. This is not necessarily the popular thing to do. The reason we are motivated to do it, believe it can be done, and is the right thing to do, is because we believe that it is the truth. We believe that the message of Jesus Christ is God's word made flesh, but more than that. We believe that the mainline Protestant perspective is an important and significant part of God's message to the church today. Mainline Protestant churches have brought some clear understanding to the scope of the Christian faith that must not be lost in the midst of the changing church scene.

Several years ago, the Tulsa economy was in shambles—major oil companies were moving away, high-tech companies were going under, and unemployment was rapidly rising. There was anger, frustration, and bewilderment. In response, Christ Church organized a job support ministry. Classes were organized to help in the job search. A support group was put together. Resources were mobilized by the church for jobs that were available. In the course of helping meet that need, people across the community who were out of work came to the job support group, came to the church, found the power of Christ, joined the church, *and* found help in their job search.

Because Christ has called us to be a community of care, that care responds to every area of need. In the first Iraq war, Desert Storm, and the second, Christ United Methodist Church in Tulsa became the center of support for families whose members were being deployed to Iraq. On weeknights, meeting rooms were filled with people talking and sharing. Experts from the community came to provide help, aid, counseling, and a variety of support. The shock of the deployment to the families was met with the love of Christlike care. Hundreds of people were in the building. Television cameras were telling the story of help. People came not only to the support group, but also to worship and Sunday school. People who were being helped and people who wanted to be a part of a church that was helping came to worship, and many joined.

The Gift of Grace

Our major gift is a gift of grace. Too often, our brothers and sisters in other fellowships begin with a focus upon sin and guilt. Certainly, many people are motivated by sin and guilt, and certainly there are reasons for us to feel the pressure of sin and to feel caught in the trap of guilt; and yet, many people are not led to Christ through guilt. Many, in fact, are driven from the gospel. Many people caught in the manipulations of the old kind of fear, guilt, hellfire, and brimstone made the decision not to follow Christ and never to go back to church again. The gospel of grace is desperately needed. The Wesleyan faith was a faith built on a concept of God's powerful grace. The Methodist movement is a movement of forgiveness and love that is needed in this new foreign land. We are a church that focuses upon real behavior; we do not just brag on our piety. Jesus said at the end of the Sermon on the Mount that "not everyone who says to me, 'Lord, Lord,' will enter the kingdom of heaven, but only the one who does the will of my Father in heaven" (Matthew 7:21). We are called to be the doers.

Ted went reluctantly to our church to attend a divorce adjustment workshop. For years, he had been one of the leaders in a local fundamental Bible church. With his divorce, he had essentially been thrown out of the church and rejected by his old friends. In his anger, Ted had wandered without a church, without a fellowship, condemned. To go back to church again seemed so painful, and yet he was hurting so much because of the divorce, he went to the workshop. Instead of being condemned for his sin and mistakes, instead of being told how awful he was, he was told that God loves each of us and that God cares for us, even when we have done the wrong thing or gone through the worst tragedy of our life or suffered through the pain of rejection. He was told that God loves us and that Jesus Christ died for all of us. That amazing grace brought the angry, closed-minded, guilt-filled Christian back to God. The power of a church that would love Ted and not condemn him has led that man to be a strong leader in the "grace" church. He knows the difference between a grace church and a non-grace church. His beliefs are unwavering. He knows the truth of God's love. When this former closed-minded conservative is asked what happened to him, Ted's answer is simple, "This church saved my life."

We need to understand that it is that kind of conviction about what we are doing that should drive us to care more and to work more intensely. The "grace" churches must begin a new season of enthusiasm about their purpose. We should be rapidly growing, not rapidly declining. Hurting people are desperate for the message of grace.

Jesus Christ gave his life for our salvation. His death on the cross is the ultimate message of love. His atonement for our sins is his act of meeting our most basic needs, which are forgiveness, truth, salvation, and purpose.

Follow Jesus

The belief that calls us to lead others to Christ is built simply upon understanding, upon a basic commitment to Jesus Christ as Lord, and a commitment to follow him. We understand that what he taught us was to love God and to love our neighbor as ourselves. In doing that, Jesus made it clear what it is to be his follower. He said that if we follow, we will live. The theology of basic commitment and belief begins with the belief that this is the truth; it is the right thing. We know that the simple statement of loving God and loving our neighbor as ourselves summarizes the answer to humankind's longing and hurt. To believe in needs-based evangelism is to believe that that's the right message to meet the desperate needs of our society. "What would Jesus do?" becomes our slogan, not because it is on our jewelry, but because it is true. In

1 Peter 2:21, we are reminded that we are called because Christ suffered for us, to meet our basic need. Christ set the example that we should "follow in his steps."

Charles Sheldon, in 1896, wrote the book *In His Steps* and in it laid out a practical, behavioral theology that is the truth of the gospel. James wrote that "faith without works is . . . dead" (James 2:26). This is the message of Jesus that can meet the needs of our society.

Mary brought to the Evangelism Committee a program to provide food to those who have low income. Some on the committee said, too quickly, "How could just giving someone food lead them to Christ?" Mary said simply, "Because it is the right thing to do. It's what Jesus taught, and we believe that if we can help people through giving them a meal, we can also help them find Jesus." It is the truth. In order to help the local church stay on target with needs-based evangelism, it must be more than a pragmatic evangelism program. It needs to be deeply imbedded in a belief system of the congregation so the church understands that this is who we are. This is what we believe in.

The Christyle

In His Steps is a simple book that outlines what might be called behavioralistic Christianity. That is, using 1 Peter 2:21 as a scriptural model, we follow in the steps of Jesus. Sheldon's book is still a best-seller. The twenty-first-century world needs a Christian behavior that is clear, to the point, and simple. We live in such a complex world that we need to begin with some basic ideas in order to address this complexity. Sheldon suggested a simple idea that works in every circumstance. Sheldon's stories in his book were practical, usable, involving real struggles for morality, integrity, and authenticity. The concept is simple. Follow in the steps of Jesus; ask what would Jesus do. In many ways, this concept has been trivialized by the "WWJD?" mentality displayed on jewelry, decorations, and everything from bookends to Bible covers. As trivial as this has become, it is still one of the most profound ideas presented by Christian theologians.

"What *would* Jesus do?" Jesus' answer in Luke 10 and Matthew 22 is the Great Commandment: to love God and love your neighbor as yourself. This sums up in a clear way what it means to follow in the steps of Jesus. The belief system of a Christian is one built upon the integrity of doing our best to follow what Christ taught and where he leads. Jesus taught us, as recorded at the end of Matthew's Gospel and in the book of Acts, that we are simply to make disciples.

Early in my pastorate at Christ United Methodist Church in Tulsa, we struggled to define who we were. The church was in a desperate time of financial need. Attendance had declined. The congregation had been in a church-wide fight several years before, and I came as a young pastor seeking answers about what to do. My grandmother had given me, as a high school senior, the book *In His Steps*. The summer of my becoming pastor of Christ Church, it seemed that there were no answers. Then I remembered Sheldon's book. It became the reading for the congregation. I preached from the Gospels, helping us struggle with what it would mean to follow in the steps of Jesus. By Christmas of that first year, the church had made the same promise that the members of the congregation in the book *In His Steps* made. That is, they would ask what would Jesus do in every decision. We called that theology the "Christyle," that is, doing and behaving in the style of life that was modeled after Jesus Christ. In our search for usable theology for a complex, highly complicated twenty-first-century world, the simple ideas of Charles Sheldon's book may be the springboard to a needs-based evangelism that is built upon a clear belief, a simple usable theology that can call for uncompromising commitment to follow the teachings of Jesus.

The Rules

The theological basis for an effective, authentic Christ-centered belief system is found in the answer that Jesus gave the lawyer in Luke 10. The lawyer's inquiring of Jesus, "What must I do to inherit eternal life?" represents the same questioning mentality that is found in the twenty-first century. The secular shopper today is asking, "What difference does it make?" "What do you believe in?" "What does this Jesus Christ teach?" "What are the essentials?" "What are the basics?" In the midst of a confusing world where the basics seem to most people to be so hard to understand, Christians present themselves with such diversity that we have often lost our effectiveness. The answer that Jesus gave to the lawyer is our answer. The Great Commandment represents the foundation of who we are, whether we see ourselves, theologically, as evangelical, progressive, moderate, or liberal. These commandments are the basis of who we are. To follow Jesus means we believe in loving God with our whole being and in loving our neighbor as ourselves.

In the church I serve as pastor, we have diagrammed the Great Commandment with an equilateral triangle. In the center of the triangle is the word *Love*. At the top is *God*, and each of the other corners are *Others* and *Self*. It is interesting that the commandment to show love to God is often biblically expressed by showing love to others. The commandment to show love to others is inept unless we have a sense of dignity ourselves. The dignity that comes from God's great promise to us is that we are loved. We can love ourselves because we know that God so loved the world that he sent his only Son, not to condemn the world, but that the world through him might be saved. The message of the Christian faith, as found in the Great Commandment, begins with the assumption that God loves us first. This grace theology allows us to be loving to others. It opens the door to healthy self-esteem.

This grace theology leads us to worship God unquestionably. The Great Commandment provides a systematic way to understand what it is that the Christian does. The Christian is loving, totally committed to God, totally committed in showing love to others, and lives with a sense of confidence and pride in oneself. The concept of love as taught by Jesus is expressed in justice, evangelism, care, and all forms of ministry. We are concerned about a person's life, lifestyle, well-being, and salvation. There is no separation among issues of social justice, social concerns, evangelism, or salvation. They are found in the same commandment: "Love your neighbor." Paul says in Romans 13, all can be summarized in that simple concept. Needs-based evangelism is based on that love.

John 3:16 has been the favorite scripture of Christians for centuries. The Twenty-third Psalm is the most chosen scripture to be repeated and read under any circumstance. Both of these proclaim the same theological idea, and that is that God loves us. The grace of God that John expresses in the third chapter of his Gospel is to let us understand that God loves us. Paul affirms that same theology in Romans 8 as he tells us that "nothing can separate us from the love of God," the understanding that while we were yet sinners, Christ died for us. Paul proclaims in Romans 3 a theological explanation, not only for the coming of Christ, but also for his death upon the cross for our salvation. We are loved. It is because of that love we can love others. It is because of that love we are motivated to be a movement of change, a radical army of those who have come to bring peace.

The Mission Statement

Written as the church's missional statement, put on the stationery, described with metaphors and symbols, the mission statement of the church needs to be rehearsed time and time again. Our task is to lead people to Christ. Our method is helping them to know of God's love. Our strategy is being there to help wherever the hurt is.

Congregations can develop a clear way of mobilizing the church's energy by putting their sense of mission into a statement. Corporate America has developed a sophistication in preparing goal statements, mission statements, and objectives to mobilize the energy of a corporation. A congregation should have a clear mission statement that affirms the priority of the commitment to follow Jesus and make disciples. Needs-based evangelism can be clearly and biblically the concluding statement in any missional affirmation of a local congregation. The power of a mission statement that includes need-based evangelism is reminding the congregation over and over of its commitment, to meet needs and witness to the gospel. It becomes a leverage to help skeptics be clear about where the church is going. If used in sermons, Sunday school lessons, publicity, and brochures, it becomes a way to remind everyone of what direction the church is going. The objectives of the mission statement need to be in the sermons, newsletter announcements, and other public statements. This will remind the congregation over and over of its direction and mission. Most congregations need to be reminded of their mission at least once a month, if not every Sunday.

We were having a meeting to decide what the church symbol should look like. Every organization and corporate group has some kind of logo. Our church has three crosses on its tower, so it was suggested that the three crosses represent the three parts of the Great Commandment, to love God and to love your neighbor and to love yourself. It was a great way to use an existing church fixture to represent our commitment. But someone said that wasn't enough. There needed to be some sign of action, showing that we really want to help in reaching new people for Christ. After lots of debate and discussion, someone suggested that what we needed was a sign of movement; and so they drew an arrow right through the middle of the three crosses. We want to be a church that is helping, that is making our city better, a church that is leading people to the truth of God. That symbol, those biblical words, are repeated over and over and over.

The churches that are growing across America have clear mission statements that encapsulate their vision of meeting social and personal needs with the love of Jesus Christ. Our belief is that faith and works cannot be separated, that evangelism and social and personal needs are the same. We believe that through meeting needs, we can make disciples of Jesus Christ.

Our beliefs direct our behavior. We must be clear about our conviction to follow the Great Commandment as Jesus taught, to help others like the good Samaritan to follow the Great Commission, and to show our faith as we seek to help others.

CHAPTER 4

HOW TO BE A GOOD SAMARITAN CHURCH

A Simple Definition of Church

It was one of those periodic times when the local church leadership wanted to have an extensive planning time—setting goals, rewriting the mission statement, evaluating what had been done in the past, looking for trouble spots in the church organization—that kind of thing. The consultant they had hired to help them asked the group to make a list of needs. It was the third planning session. They had done a session on reviewing the history of the church. They had done a very comprehensive session on evaluating the general church program, facilities, staffing, and such as that. Now the consultant asked them simply to list needs. Sheets of newsprint were up. People worked in small groups. They made a list of the major needs of the community, the major needs of families, the major needs of individuals. The room was plastered with a litany of all kinds of needs.

At a point about halfway through the allotted time for that Saturday afternoon session, Bill, one of the long-time, rather negative members of the congregation stopped the whole process as he asked simply, "I don't understand why we're doing this. What does it matter to a church, all these things that are going on in our society? We all know what the needs are. We know about family problems, divorce, economy, depression, and drugs. I don't see how this gets us anywhere. Why are we so concerned about this list of needs or problems? I thought our job was to be Christian and follow Jesus and proclaim the gospel. You know, to be Christian witnesses." Several people in the room joined in with Bill's comments, and it looked as though the meeting was about to come apart. The pastor, not knowing what the consultant had in mind with this exercise, turned to the consultant and asked simply, "Can you help?" The consultant walked across the room and picked up a Bible off a shelf covered with out-of-date Sunday school literature and old hymnals. He turned to Luke 10 and began to read the story of the good Samaritan. When he finished reading this story, he quoted Jesus, saying, "Go thou and do likewise." The consultant said, "If your church is going to do what Jesus taught, you have to be a good Samaritan church."

Maybe that's an oversimplification, and yet, that statement is the key to being an authentic church. The story of the good Samaritan is a superb story that describes the struggle we have in meeting needs. The story could be outlined simply by saying that the good Samaritan first *noticed*—he saw somebody was in trouble, saw something was wrong. Second, he *stopped*. As busy as he was, as tempted as he must have been to move on like the others did, he stopped. Third, he *helped*. He helped in a way that was appropriate. It involved a risk, but it was effective. Fourth, he got *personally involved*. He put the guy on his own animal. He disregarded the danger that was present. And fifth, he *followed up*. He said he would come back by. He said he would help further if needed. That's a clear example of what we're called to do if we're going to follow the teachings of Jesus and meet real needs.

In Matthew 25, Jesus describes the judgment day as a time of separating the sheep from the goats. The standard of whether or not you get to be a sheep is whether you help other people. Helping and caring is what Jesus taught!

Finding the Needs in Your Community

If we are to be a good Samaritan church, we must understand what the needs are in our community. If we are to be a church using needs-based evangelism as a way to reach new people for Christ, we need to be clear, careful, and enthusiastic about meeting needs.

It begins with using the best knowledge of the local congregation to ascertain what those needs are. Oftentimes, the best knowledge is from people in the group. Most members of the local church are aware of what is going on in the community. Sometimes it's as simple as asking everyone to make a list of five needs within the community, then a second list of five needs of individuals, and then maybe a third list of five needs of families. As you make these lists and bring them together with a group of ten to fifty people, you get a pretty good analysis of what's really going on in your community. It becomes a kind of focus group to determine what the needs are.

Second, there are experts who can provide information, experts that are part of the local institutions. Congregations wanting to have additional information on needs within the community should contact public school leaders, social workers, government officials, hospital administrators, local chambers of commerce, community planning committees, and many other groups. The task is to find what the understood needs are. There are many techniques for examining community needs, and planning sessions as mentioned above and asking for experts to come and speak and review the needs already expressed in the local church are particularly effective.

A third way to become aware of individual needs is to be aware of the particular needs within the congregation. As you survey those needs with questionnaires, discussion groups, and other gatherings, you can find within the congregation where there is an interest. This becomes the basis of a support group or study group. This third way of needs assessment responds to the needs that are already evident. You will find if it is a problem within the congregation, there are probably resources within the congregation to meet the needs. To do needs-based evangelism you need not only a need that the congregation is interested in, but also people who can provide training, support, and other answers for those with that need. For example, a program of developing a widow/widowers support group will not work well unless there are widows and widowers who are willing to be a part of developing the group. Another way to describe needs-based evangelism is "niche marketing." Where we have the best resources to meet a particular need, focus on that need. Local churches cannot meet all the needs, but they can find niches. A church with lots of young children might have the resources to meet the needs and do ministry to young families and young children. A congregation that has a passion for single moms because several leaders are single moms is in a beautiful position to mobilize energy and interest to meet the needs of other single moms.

At Christ Church, our Divorce Ministry began because members of the congregation who had gone through divorce and secular therapy felt as if the church ought to offer faith-based help. They conceptualized the idea of a divorce adjustment workshop. They did the work to put it together. And as people came to be a part of the workshop and found help, they stayed and helped do the next workshop.

A fourth way of ascertaining needs is responding to a crisis. In our communities and families, there are always events and situations that develop such that they bring the awareness of particular needs clearly to the mind of everyone. On September 11, 2001, churches all across America had prayer meetings and developed support groups and systems to deal with the fear and frustration of this nation. A county seat church in Virginia experienced suicide in a graphic way when one of the leading members of the church committed suicide on the steps of the church. The church realized that depression, mental illness, and suicide prevention were important. Programs were put in place. The church provided ministries and counseling that not only helped persons through an immediate crisis, but oftentimes, for years after. For a church *not* to respond to crisis is insensitive, not noticing, and not caring. Needs-based evangelism means we must be ready to respond to whatever the crisis is.

A church in a high-crime neighborhood organized a neighborhood watch, neighborhood monitoring, youth programs, and youth employment services to help deal with the crisis of violence in their streets. As a result, people became involved in the gospel of Jesus Christ.

Niche Marketing and Your Resources

In Matthew 25, Jesus told the story of the talents to help us understand that we are to use the gifts that God has given us in the best way we can. In the story, the three recipients of the talents received different amounts. So it is with local churches. Some churches have lots of resources and some have few. That doesn't matter. The issue is to use your resources well.

Niche marketing has to do with what resources the local congregation has. Effective ministry is done when there is a basis of strength from which to do that ministry. If there are lots of young families in your congregation, you are probably in a good place to reach out to more young families. If you have a large group of young twenty-year-olds who are going to college in your town, you might be able to be one of the few churches with an effective twenties ministry.

Birds of a feather do flock together. There is strength in numbers. Consider which generation your church is strongest in. And consider that that might be the generation that you seek to meet their needs.

There is a contrary theory to this, and that is, if you are not strong in an area, that's the area you ought to relate to. That is to get your church balanced. That's probably not a valid theory. A more valid theory is, even though you do not have a large number of people in a certain area, if you have persons highly committed to that area, it can become an effective priority.

I know a church that is predominately boomers. The older boomers in the church had been complaining that their children weren't coming to church anymore. Their kids went to college and quit going to church. Kids came home from college and still didn't go to church. When the church planning committee was working on a priority for an area of ministry, several of those boomers who were concerned about their kids said we needed to have a program to reach those in their young twenties. The resource was not the number of people in the congregation, but the strength of commitment to that area of ministry.

Transitions Are Niche Opportunities

Transition time between generations can become major opportunities to minister to needs. One of the difficult things in human life is moving from one phase to the next: getting married, becoming a parent for the first time, finding yourself as a noncustodial parent, becoming an empty nester, moving into retirement, caring for an aging parent, preparing for the death of someone you love. All these transitions are areas of great need for the person of faith and for the most secular individual in our community.

Organized ministries and support groups can be significant in helping people make the ultimate decisions of faith. Even preaching in worship services that focuses upon transition times can become the new schedule for the liturgical year. Needs-based evangelism can simply be based upon the transition times in life. People most often make decisions for Christ when they are going through transitions. Most do not make decisions about commitment and directions in life when everything is going well. We make those decisions when we are in the midst of stress and difficulty. When the church is there to help and share the gospel at the point of their greatest need, people respond, because during those times people are most open.

Jill's youngest son, Andrew, was having serious problems in the seventh grade. Middle school was tough. Social pressures were great. Andrew was doing poorly in school. His behavior was very irresponsible. Jill's husband had tried to find answers. He had talked to their pediatrician and local therapist. When the church across the street from the school announced on their front marquee that they were having a class for parents of kids in junior high, Tom and Jill were there in plenty of time to find their way in a church they had never been in. It took a few moments to find a good seat and to be a part of the training program they knew they needed.

In the weeks that followed and as the classes proceeded, they became acquainted with the other people in the class. They realized that the church had a great program for their teenager. They visited worship several times and became part of a support group for parents. Within six months, things were better with their son. He was now involved in the church and active in the youth program. They had joined the church and were helping organize the next parenting training program. This is a simple story of how needs evangelism works.

The need for knowledge of English in our community is great among Hispanic people. Several women who taught English as a second language volunteered to offer a free class on Sunday evening. The class began to grow. It became evident that as Hispanic people learned the English language, some of them were interested in the church that was teaching the language. They were interested enough to go to a Spanish Sunday school class and maybe be a part of a new Hispanic congregation. The beginning of the new Hispanic satellite congregation was started by simply offering English classes.

Needs and Inviting

The concept of needs-based evangelism is to respond to the needs that exist within the community and to provide the answers of the gospel of Jesus Christ to meet those needs. If we meet the needs lovingly, the invitation to know Jesus Christ can be made clear. The gospel is proclaimed in the course of meeting the needs. Then some of the people being helped will make a decision for Christ and become a part of the church.

One of the struggles that Christians often have is how to make the invitation in the midst of meeting a need. Sally was a child psychologist conducting a class on parenting for her church. As she finished the opening session, she simply invited everyone to be in church the next Sunday. She made a reference to the sermon topic and how that fit in to the needs of parenting. Next week in the class, she invited someone from the youth department to come and share about the youth program. In one of the sessions, she gave her own testimony of how much her relationship with God mattered. She worked with the active members of the church in her parenting class, asking them to sit by the visitors and to build relationships and friendships with the people that she knew had no church and were, in some way, shopping. In a class with thirty people, of whom ten had no church affiliation, by the end of the parenting class, seven of the ten were actively involved in the church.

The invitation can be made by simply building a relationship or friendship. Relational evangelism is natural in the midst of helping a person. Helping can be the first step that can lead to a friendship of love. People can experience the witness of Jesus Christ through the example of those who are helping. As they see Christ in others, so they will be attracted to the way of the church.

Oftentimes, in the midst of meeting needs, there will be questions asked about the church, about the church's beliefs. Giving information, sharing, or explaining can be a beautiful way to invite, inform, and help someone become a disciple of Christ. Many times, in the midst of a helping workshop, a teaching situation, or a support group, a committed Christian has an opportunity to tell his or her story. Without being arrogant or holier than thou, a simple story can be a powerful way of witnessing. Of course, there must finally be the invitation, that is, to invite the person who has received help through the ministry to come and worship on Sunday morning or join a Sunday school class or church event. Opportunities to invite in a needs-based congregation will be numerous. The final invitation that is a part of needs-based ministry, however, is inviting a person to become a follower of Jesus Christ. Usually, it is done after a period of building trust and relationship. Usually, it is done in the midst of setting the example of what it is to be a Christian in your own life. But, at some point, the sharing of the truth of the gospel needs to be accompanied with an invitation and encouragement for the person to commit his or her life to Christ, to find the power of Jesus Christ, and to become a part of his church.

Celebrating Being the Good Samaritan Church

Good Samaritan churches must continually teach the congregation and emphasize the importance of meeting needs. Niche marketing can be celebrated in the general announcements of the church, bulletins, and newsletters and certainly from the pulpit. As stories about needs are part of sermons, and as ministries to meet particular needs are publicized, they become a way of helping church members see their own particular ministry niche.

One of the principal ways in which the whole congregation understands the priority of evangelism, the concept of being a good Samaritan church, the theology of following the teachings of Jesus, the belief in the priority of grace, is that the church celebrates who it is over and over. This may be done through the church's mission statement printed in the bulletin every week. It should be printed often with explanation of the church's logo so the children as well as the adults understand what kind of church they are part of and how the logo symbolizes their church.

The celebration can be part of a multiplicity of events, workshops, and ministry programs during which individuals are recognized for their good work. An important part of the celebration is always a sense of joy. Too often, the imperative to be a witness becomes almost negative, a painful, heavy burden to carry. Jesus spoke of his burden being light, and so it can be with being a good Samaritan church. A good Samaritan church is not meant to be bitter and hard, but satisfying, joyful, and rewarding every step of the way. Great worship, good fellowship, singing and laughter, handshakes and hugs need to be parts of a church that cares and reaches new people for Christ.

Experiment

Certainly, good Samaritan congregations must be willing to experiment because needs-based evangelism is so complex and involves so many feelings and so many people. There will be times that things don't work, that people don't respond. But there will be other times when things go better than your church ever dreamed possible. A good Samaritan congregation needs to be willing to experiment, evaluate, and make corrections and changes. Some of the basic niches have to do with family life, parenting, singles ministry, divorced persons, widows and widowers, job searching, making vocational transition, people suffering from depression, and people seeking to overcome financial difficulty. These are just a few of the niches a local congregation could take on using the resources of the members and the opportunities to reach new people through meeting needs.

CHAPTER 5

NEEDS-BASED THINKING

Refreshing New Thinking

For the last several years in many, many churches across America, there has been growing pessimism. We have seen secular influence grow, and we have lost influence in our communities. The independent Bible churches and charismatic fellowships have become the largest churches in our community. We need a new way of thinking. To embrace needs-based evangelism is to embrace the new possibility, a way in which we can naturally reach new people for Jesus Christ. It is an exciting new way of thinking that is based upon an old basic theology of the church. Needs-based thinking provides an opportunity for people to see that we can change lives, we can change the church, and we can change the world by doing the basic thing that we know best and that's helping other people.

It is true that larger churches are getting larger and smaller churches are getting smaller, and many, many churches are feeling overwhelmed by the mega-churches in our society. The competition with these churches that seem to have an endless supply of money seems to be overwhelming, and yet, with needs-based evangelism, there can be real success and a new "possibility-thinking" present. We need a new way of thinking so we can do effective evangelism and make a difference. We need to believe that, no matter what our size and situation, we can be successful. This is basic to believing in needs-based evangelism. It is biblical, it is authentic, and it works.

The Basic Thinking

The basic premise of needs-based evangelism is, first, as followers of Jesus Christ and committed Christians, we are called to do two things: make disciples of Jesus Christ, and help persons in need. To separate this into two is false, for needs-based evangelism is built upon the premise that if you meet needs, if it is done authentically, we lead people to Christ.

The second basic concept is that one of the reasons needs-based evangelism works well is that the gospel is brought to people's lives at the time they are interested, vulnerable, and open. In that way, it is authentic in terms of care and evangelism.

Third, needs-based evangelism is built upon the concept of grace—that is, it begins not from anger or guilt or judgment, but from love and care and sensitivity and concern. It can only be done effectively in churches whose theology is one of grace rather than judgment. Grace and judgment are part of all theological perspectives, but needs-based evangelism works when grace is the beginning perspective, the dominating perspective.

The fourth concept of needs-based evangelism is that it must be done as part of a whole church's self-understanding. It must come out of a biblical commitment to do what Jesus taught. The Great Commandment, the Great Commission, the story of the judgment day in Matthew 25, the instructions in James 2 and 1 John 4, all provide the theological and biblical basis for needs-based evangelism.

Finally, for a church to do needs-based evangelism effectively, there must be consensus within the church—that is, the church must have written a mission statement and developed slogans and metaphors 'to describe their commitment to being a good Samaritan church. This must be taught and lifted up to the entire congregation over and over and over in order for the entire system to work. Repetition and redundancy become key to that affirmation of purpose. The way in which that is taught is not only through a cognitive explaining that it is the right thing to do, but also by affirming the congregation whenever the church responds in that way. It is to give the reward of affirmation openly to members of the congregation who do the action of Christ and to minimize the recognition of action that is simply local church maintenance instead of mission.

We had celebrated and affirmed our mission statement over and over. The ideas were simple: follow in the steps of Jesus, commit to the Great Commandment and the Great Commission, and understand that we are called to be a good Samaritan church. Diana was trying to make it simple and easy to remember. She suggested that the heart of the matter was the Great Commandment, and you could diagram the Great Commandment with a triangle. On the blackboard, she drew a triangle; she put *LOVE* across the middle of the triangle, *GOD* at the top, *OTHERS* on one corner, and *SELF* on the other. This equilateral triangle was, for Diana, a clear representation of what it meant to follow Jesus—to be a good Samaritan church, to respond to needs. The triangle has been used over and over by many individuals seeking to find a simple way to clarify our mission statement.

Compassionate Thinking

So much of society is self-centered, arrogant, and pessimistic. It is time for the Christian to be touched by the power of the Holy Spirit and to understand the meaning of God's love for us all in Jesus Christ. In John 4, the Bible explains to us that God showed his love for us in Jesus Christ, calling us to show compassion to others. We need to think like the good Samaritan, noticing, caring, helping, and helping some more. The Bible also teaches us in the story of the judgment day in Matthew 25 that if we will act with compassion, we will experience the presence of Christ in our lives. It can be the most exciting, joyful, satisfying experience of our lives.

Each of the scriptures above point out the heart of the gospel—whether it's Jesus explaining that only the compassionate will be judged as sheep on judgment day or

John making it clear that, unless we show love to others, God is not in our life. Jesus' story of the good Samaritan is one that cannot be missed, because it is a simple, clear example of what it is to be loving. It is a way of thinking. It is a way to act.

She was new to the church, single, and in her fifties. As she became acquainted with the theology of love, she asked a simple question: Why can't we organize a support group for grandparents raising their grandkids? That's what she was doing—that is, raising her grandson—and it just seemed natural that the church would want to be there to help. Compassionate thinking is natural for those who follow Jesus.

Thinking Big

The problem with so much of the church's attitude about life is that we think so small. We refuse to believe that we can change people, we can change the world, or we can change our own way of living. It is time for us to gain a new enthusiasm about life and a new enthusiasm about what the church can do today. We have covered our frustration and bewilderment with an addiction to pessimism that has become our only way of thinking. It is time for us to think big, to think that the church can grow.

Ten years ago in Tulsa, Oklahoma, a new church was started with a handful of people. Today, it is one of the largest churches in America because those in the church thought big and believed that they could make a difference in the Tulsa community. That same experience is happening over and over in America, where independent Bible churches and charismatic fellowships are experiencing significant rapid growth.

At Mayfield United Methodist Church in Cleveland, Ohio, the church realized that the facilities simply were not large enough. They needed to relocate. Even though it was difficult with community laws and regulations, under Don Cummings's leadership, the church made the hard transition, thinking about new possibilities, and they moved. Sometimes, to think big means a move; other times it means staying. Asbury United Methodist Church in Tulsa relocated and jumped from two thousand to four thousand in attendance. Christ United Methodist Church made the decision to stay in midtown Tulsa, where the population is declining somewhat and parking is limited, and moved from an average attendance of seven hundred to sixteen hundred.

Mainline Protestant churches need to begin to think big. Instead of limiting what we can do, limiting what we can dream, we need to realize that we can make a difference. If we believe in the gospel, then we need to believe that lives can be changed and that we can reach more and more people for Jesus Christ. The more people we reach, the more good we can do, and the more soldiers we have for the kingdom of sharing God's love. Meeting needs means growth for God's church.

Be Open to Learning from Others

One of the old styles of thinking that is so limiting is that we think good ideas only come from one source, that inspiration is found only in certain long-term institutional forms. With the high level of change that is happening in our society, we must understand that new ideas come from all directions. It is time for us to be open to that creativity that God has placed in so many different settings. One of the primary ways in which mainline churches today can think differently is by learning from others. Learn from the mega-church. Learn from the Bible fellowships. Learn from the charismatic groups. Learn from business. Learn from industry. Learn from the marketing gurus in our society. God has given all this knowledge for us. We have isolated ourselves from the opportunities to learn how to reach people for Jesus Christ because we have not been willing to look at the many sources of education possible.

Today's American clergy who are a part of churches that are growing generally all have the same characteristics: being hungry to learn a new idea, attending workshops, and visiting other churches. Adam Hamilton, when his growing United Methodist church in Kansas City came to a plateau early in his ministry, decided that he would take the entire summer off as a sabbatical and visit large growing churches all across America, to learn from them. The Large Church Initiative of The United Methodist Church is built purely on the idea of peer learning. The Willow Creek Association has grown rapidly based upon the ability of Willow Creek to offer valid learning experiences that work. It is time for us to think differently, to learn from all the ways that God is teaching.

Think Recruit

For the church to be strong, for us to do needs-based evangelism, the laity must do it. It is not a simple gimmicky program. It is not an activity that lasts for a few days. It is a continuous program of caring and helping and following up. In order to do this, we need to recruit, recruit, and recruit. We need to train, encourage, support, affirm, congratulate, and recruit again. The church of the laity is the answer for the needs-based church. Needs-based evangelism will not work unless we have an army of men and women, youth and children, who are willing to help and share the gospel as they help.

In recent years, it has been popular for churches to try harder to help individuals find their particular place of involvement in the local church. We have all kinds of testing to help people find their place in the church. We offer great programs to train people to do particular jobs in the church. Needs-based evangelism simply asks people to be willing to try. Of course, there must be training. Of course, many of the needs-based evangelism activities need highly skilled and carefully trained leaders, and yet, so often, the largest part of meeting needs is simply a willingness to spend some time and some love in order to help.

When the church sets the goal of being a church of the laity, when meeting needs is a priority, and this is clearly based upon commitment to Jesus Christ, recruitment is not necessarily a begging and manipulation of church members; but it's a natural way of giving an opportunity to express the joy of being a part of the church. If announcements about needs that need to be met are printed in the bulletin, organizational meetings are open to all church members, and newsletter articles tell where help is needed, then, most of the time—if the proper concepts have been embedded in the life and thinking of the church—recruitment is natural and easy. Involvement becomes the way of being the church. One of the dangers of the church as it gets larger and hires staff is that the members begin to think that they're not needed, that people have been hired to do the job. When attendance grows enough that two or three staff can be hired, it's imperative that the local church continue to emphasize that the church is made up of not a few staff, but all the members doing God's work together. Needs ministry as the basis of recruitment becomes natural to the needs perception of the congregation.

Rita loved art. She had come to the church through an invitation from a friend. She had liked the church in a variety of ways, but there didn't seem to be any way that she could express her love for art within the life of the church. So she volunteered to organize art classes, to put on a Christian art show, and to offer classes and programs for children, youth, and adults who were interested in expressing their faith through art. The whole ministry was organized without any recruitment, but because there was a need and a willingness of the church to meet the need.

Involvement in the life of the church needs to be easy and responsive to the needs of the congregation. Some tasks can be as simple as helping with mailings or serving ice cream at a fellowship activity. Others can be complex, involving working with individuals who are being released from prison or organizing a support group for parents of teenagers. The beautiful thing about involvement is that it gives opportunity for expression of the faith, meeting needs, and great fellowship.

The church had organized a neighborhood walk—that is, we were walking the neighborhood around the church to leave flyers and bulletins on the doors of the various people in the neighborhood. For some, it was a great Saturday morning walk. For others, it was an act of personal commitment and dedication. And for some others, it was an opportunity to do something simple to help on a Saturday and to feel good about their faith. For most, it was an opportunity for fellowship and to meet a real need.

Elmo had lost his wife several months before, and, on that Saturday, he showed up with a group of members who were going to walk the neighborhood around the church and leave flyers and invitations to activities. He was alone, but he was loyal to the church. The leader of the neighborhood walk asked that everybody go in pairs, and so people began to pair up in a variety of ways. At the end, Elmo was left standing with several other people as they were organizing to go. Those who were left, in a sense, alone, did not come with someone else, or did not know someone else in the group. And so Craig, who was organizing the walk, just put them together in pairs. It just happened that Elmo's partner was a widowed lady who was part of the widow and widower support group. They walked the neighborhood and became friends. A year later, they were married. There are all kinds of joys and benefits of being a participant in the work of God's loving church.

Innovate, Innovate, Scrounge

Needs-based evangelism is costly. It costs time, materials, and money. To compete in today's American society, we must have quality church facilities, quality worship, and quality staff. The struggle that most churches are having in doing this is that they are limited on funds. We are small because we don't have money. We don't have money because we are small. The only way out of this trap is to innovate, to find new ways, to ask people to bring resources, whatever resources they can find in order to meet the needs. Society is filled with all kinds of resources. We simply have not thought of creative ways to access those resources.

When people believe in the mission of the church, they are willing to make gifts. Gifts can come not only in the forms of money and time, but also in other forms—such as in gifts of cars and boats, carpet, desks, computers, or office supplies. If we provide the opportunity, people want to respond where they know that needs are really being met.

We were building a new wing at the church. We wanted it to be tiled with ceramic tile. We were out of money to buy that quality tile. A member of the congregation mentioned that his company had last year's stock and that they had changed the design and wanted to get rid of the material. The material was donated. The church gave the company a receipt for the donation. The company had the tax advantage. The church has the tile, and the gospel has a beautiful building.

We need to think creatively in every kind of way to find the resources. Teams of laity need to gather together and pray and dream and share and brainstorm about ways to get the financial resources and the materials necessary to do needs-based evangelism. At the same time, as churches begin to grow and become effective in reaching new people for Christ, the resources of finances will also begin to grow. When we make no apologies about our desire to reach new people for Christ and our imperative to help those who are in need, we should make no apologies about asking for the tithe and more. The ironic thing is that instead of people bemoaning the church's overemphasis on money, they are enthusiastic about wanting to help when the hurt is there. In my ministry, the story is repeated over and over, that when the church does authentic helping, people rush to be given the opportunity to help financially.

Oftentimes, giving is stimulated by ordinary members of the church who are given an opportunity to share their commitment and their understanding of tithing and giving to the whole congregation. Testimonies work today in our "reality TV"-based society. People want to know why you give and how you give.

Tom stood and told his story to the whole congregation about the crisis that he'd gone through, losing his job, going through divorce, struggling with the finances, getting remarried, having more financial difficulties. And the heart of his story, over and over, was that he continued to tithe all the way. He shared how the church had helped meet the needs and hurts in his life and how he was committed, no matter what, to be a part of that kind of helping.

When Christ Church was working to start new churches in Russia, we were taking literally hundreds of thousands of dollars worth of medicines to Russian hospitals, and there was no limit to the donation of the medicines. When we needed Bibles and other resources, donations came readily above regular giving. When we needed gifts to give to our new friends in Russia, companies gave advertising and products that were not being sold. When people were needed to make the trip to Russia, they found the money to make the trip. When the need is there, people want to give whatever they can. It is time for us to do whatever is necessary to find the resources to make the big dream of needs-based evangelism work.

Think Joy

We are caught in the pessimistic, whining society in which everybody is griping about what is and what is not working. The media dumps into the American family a continuous diet of pessimism, negativism, and whining. The gospel of Jesus Christ is a gospel of joy. It is a gospel based upon God's love for us, knowing that we are loved by God through the gift of Jesus Christ, despite our sins. Really to do what we are taught biblically and to meet the needs of people is to find the real joy in being a Christian. The satisfaction that comes from knowing that we have done the right thing and the joy that comes from seeing people want to join and be a part of a church that cares is the source of the most basic joy anyone can find. Needs-based evangelism is joyful and fun. It is the source of deep happiness. Certainly, there are times of grave disappointment. Certainly, there are times when things do not work and people fail and our sinfulness takes over. There are times that we fight and fuss over trying to do the right thing better, and yet, basically, when we seek to be loving and to share the gospel, that love changes us and we find the joy of being his family.

The heart of much of the joy in being in a good Samaritan church is a feeling that your talents, skills, desires, and wishes are honored and that God needs you. It's built upon a concept of grace; but, in understanding that our purpose is to help others, we're doubly rewarded by being affirmed in what we have and by what we give.

Terry has gone through some difficult employment situations. He was injured on a job, and has physical difficulties because of that; and yet, he has great skills in auto mechanics. So when the church needed help in repairing its vans, Terry volunteered. Though he's been unsure about other things in his life, he knows that he's needed every week at the church to keep the vehicles running. He does it, and the reward for him is fantastic.

Bill is a retired printer, frustrated with some of the issues of aging and retirement, but when he comes to the church and donates his time as a printer, he feels dignity and a sense of worth that cannot be explained in any other way.

After the death of their daughter, a young couple in our congregation began a ministry of giving teddy bears to moms who have lost their babies. Their ministry also provides lots of comfort, materials for reading, and support. In the midst of their grief, this young couple found such magnificent joy in helping. As they give, they receive.

In each of these stories, individuals find joy, happiness, and satisfaction by helping, and, directly or indirectly, people are led to Christ.

CHAPTER 6

NEEDS-BASED ORGANIZATIONAL LIFE

Leadership

In order for an organization to be successful, there must be clear leadership. For the church to grow, for needs-based evangelism to work, the church must have leadership from staff, clergy, and the laity. Without commitment from the existing leadership, without people who take a stand, step forward, and carry the responsibility to make the plans, do the hard work, spend the hours necessary to do leadership, any program or strategy not seen as authentic will fail.

For needs-based evangelism to work, it must have the pastor first, and then key layper-sons, key staff, and other laity deeply committed. Too often, organizational development plans are put into place just because they are new, denominationally supported, popular, or easy to do without having the people who will be the committed leaders. I believe God is calling us to lead. Paul tells his church leader friend in 2 Timothy 1:7 that "God did not give us a spirit of cowardice, but rather a spirit of power and of love and of self-discipline." How the local church leaders become committed is up to both God and those whom God touches. The reading of this book, the attending of a workshop, or the discomfort in your spirit may be God's call upon your life.

God uses all kinds of ways to break through our consciousness. The question that you, the reader, must ask is, Am I willing to make a commitment? Do I believe, and am I willing to lead? For without conscious commitment and conviction to action by key people, no program will work.

The board was holding a discussion of contemporary worship. The advocates were saying it would meet the needs of many people that are now not being met through our traditional music. The arguments went back and forth. There seemed to be a clear divi-sion among the members of the council attempting to make the decision. Then Stan stood up in the middle of it. He said simply. "I don't like contemporary music. I don't want to go to a contemporary worship service. I hate drums in worship. But my church is committed to reaching people for Jesus Christ. I will support till my death anything to accomplish that. I move that we begin contemporary worship services that they might reach more people for Jesus Christ. They will meet needs that we cannot meet through the traditional service and people will be led to Jesus." And the board voted unanimously to start contemporary worship.

The Pastor and Key Laity

The organizational life of a needs-based congregation must have strong commitment and clear direction from the pastor and key staff and laity. Strong visionary leaders, good organizational managers, and, most of all, people who are committed not only to meeting needs, but also to leading people to Christ, are absolutely essential. This commitment begins with a belief clearly in the gospel of Jesus Christ, following what Jesus taught in the Great Commandment and the Great Commission. Pastors and laity must have a passion for helping individuals and leading them to become a part of the fellowship of Jesus Christ. Needs-based evangelism is exhausting, frustrating, bewildering. For it to work, key leaders must be committed. Needs-based evangelism is rewarding, exciting, satisfying, and effective. Therefore, the key leadership must reflect that excitement to the church and the nonchurch world. They must show their confidence in the gospel in the way in which they relate to the congregation and to the community. The key leaders need to be visionary, managerial, optimistic cheerleaders.

Among the team of leaders, including the staff and laity, there are many different gifts, skills, and talents. Some will be better managers, some better cheerleaders, some better organizers, and some better motivators. Each takes on his or her own task in a clear cooperative effort. However the church is organized, there must be a sense of teamwork by the key leaders.

Every Decision Is an Evangelism Decision

Every programmatic decision of the church must be evaluated on the basis of whether it will make disciples of Jesus Christ. It's easy in church organizational life to become busy with busy-ness without doing ministry and without reaching new people for Christ.

The women's group was organizing an annual fund-raiser, a craft show near Christmas. In the midst of the planning, some of the members of the team asked the serious question how these events would reach out to new people. Certainly, lots of new people come and visit the craft show, but will they be invited, and will they catch a glimpse of the kind of things the church is doing? The planners simply changed the plan. They included a hospitality section so the people who attended the show would be greeted with the spirit of love that was so present in the church. Brochures and other materials were passed out to everyone who came. A door prize was offered, and people signed up. The names became a record so that there could be further contacts, letters, and reminders sent to the individuals. The doors to the sanctuary were opened. Special concerts and other activities were held during the time of the craft show to encourage people to find out more about what was happening in the church. What was a simple means of raising funds became a means of showing hospitality and reaching new people.

In seeing that the evangelism thrust is a part of every evaluation and decision, church leadership needs to ask hard questions. Is this busy work, or is this Christ's work? Are people being helped, or are we creating people who are dependent? Is the gospel being shared, and are people receiving invitations to faith, or are we only putting on bandages? The test question for all programs is simply, Is this what Jesus would do?

Developing a Systems Approach

One of the serious problems that churches have is the inability to recognize that things aren't working well. Because "we have always done it that way," we fail to note what is really happening in our church.

Corporate America has for a long time used a systems approach. Manufacturers check how raw materials are acquired and processed on the assembly line, how delivery is done, how sales are made; and then they check the whole system to see if there are any inefficiencies, brakes, or dysfunctions within the system as a whole.

For the church, this approach means seeing the church as a dynamic system working to deliver a desired result. Churches can use a systems approach to look at and examine the whole flow of how people become involved in the church, and how persons become acquainted with the faith, how the gospel is presented in the life of the church, and how ministries of service and care are done. In analyzing the systems and by asking questions such as whether there are blocks in the system, leaks in the system, or inefficiencies in the system, you can be more solution-oriented in church organizational life.

David was excited about the number of visitors that began to come to the church after a new recovery program was instituted. As Board Chair, he was enthusiastic about the recovery ministry. Lots of people attended the support groups and recovery groups. Many of those people were visiting the church, and yet it seemed as if they would visit a couple of times and not come back. David appointed a task group to try to find out why the new visitors did not come back. As they began to analyze the system, they found the system was blocked by the lack of real hospitality in the church. The board approved and developed the needs-based ministry, yet the congregation was uncomfortable with all the new people. The system was blocked by the lack of practiced love. Sunday school classes and other groups had developed a closed system. They weren't welcoming the new people in. New Sunday school classes were organized. A program of hospitality was established. New classes were put into place. Sponsors and shepherds for the visitors were organized in order to see that the system delivered an experience of the gospel to the visitors. With all the proactive plans, still visitors did not return. Susan, a church prayer group leader, realized that much of the problem was really spiritual. There was unloving and non-Christlike closed-mindedness in the congregation. She and the prayer group leaders organized a congregational prayer program of praying for one another and for the visitors. Attitudes were converted from closed-mindedness to welcoming.

The pastor realized that many of the new people who were a part of the recovery program had slightly different needs and interests. She made a slight change in her sermon illustrations by adding a story of recovery and an honest testimony of a longtime member who had gone through some serious problems of abuse and had overcome it. She emphasized Jesus' teaching of acceptance over and over. The church began to speak about itself as an overcomers church, and the system began to work.

Systems theory understands an organization as a system, like a plumbing system in a house. Water flows for cooking and cleaning when the pipes are open and when the source is clear. If results are not being achieved, there is either a problem with the source or a problem with the piping or the flow, with the direction. Systems theory asks us to look at how things are all related to accomplish the goal, in this case, of needs-based evangelism.

Easy Decision-making

For a church to be entrepreneurial and to respond to needs with clarity and efficiency, it must have a decision-making process that does not block God's call or evangelistic opportunities.

Most mainline churches have strong democratic procedures, lots of discussion and debate. Oftentimes, the organizations have in place decision-making rules or traditions that simply stifle programs, creativity, and new ideas. Some churches have found that a discernment model is much more effective than the old discussion-and-voting-on-every-new-idea model, in which someone wins and someone loses. Discernment decision-making is a method in which the Christian organizational group uses prayer, patience, and sensitivity in making policy and program decisions. Too often, voting and debate kills an idea.

The discernment model is one of many models for making decisions. If the democratic voting method is used, it can be used with love and care. There needs to be time for prayer and open discussion. A key to decision-making is trust and a clearly understood process of making decisions. Churches are notorious for making decisions in a hard way, in a way that creates more problems than it solves, in a way that takes much too long. The decision-making for a needs-based church needs to be efficient, missional, and evangelistic. One clear attribute of any decision-making system is permission-giving.

Permission-giving

Needs-based evangelism churches enhance their growth if they develop what might be called permission-giving leadership. Permission-giving leadership can be combined with discernment or the old democratic system. It simply operates with a more empowering stance.

The church first works hard to establish clear goals and directions. The church must be self-conscious about seeing that those goals and directions are biblically sound. With the goal or mission set, then the new idea or program has permission if it fits within the goals and directions. The new program must not be in conflict with the mission. If the new program is not out of line with the church's established policies and budget, and if there are enough volunteers to do the program, then it can be done. The church council or board does not try to micromanage the new program but is openly willing to give permission if the program fits the mission. This system works well with needs-based evangelism. It is entrepreneurial and missional.

In this procedure, decision-makers are not fearful of the fact that an idea is new or if "we have never done it that way." The group trusts in the Holy Spirit, the laity, and the staff of the church, always asking the basic question, Does this new idea or program seek to accomplish the church's missional goals?

Permission-giving church organizational style encourages creativity and interest. I have watched new ministries develop and succeed, giving such satisfaction to the participants. If the goal of the church is needs-based evangelism and the organizational style is permission-giving, a plethora of needs-based evangelism programs will develop.

Melanie wanted to develop a dance class for children of single parents. Bill was interested in starting a bicycling club. Walter organized a group of grandparents rearing grandchildren. Sarah and her friends organized a Sunday school class for children who are mentally handicapped. All of these programs reached new people for Christ and the church.

Seeking to be clear about our purpose is a key to the health of the local congregation. Entrepreneurial, user-friendly decision-making is based upon being a church with a purpose that gives its members permission to develop the purpose.

One essential element in the organizational life of a mission-driven congregation that seeks to reach new people for Christ is managing the enthusiasm. For as the Spirit of God begins to work with the congregation, new ideas are created; new opportunities are opened; crazy ideas, great ideas, old ideas, and new ideas are dumped into the mix of the life of the church.

Managing Enthusiasm

One of the tasks of the leadership of the church with a clear commitment to goals is to manage the mission efficiently, effectively, and lovingly. Some new ideas won't work. Some old ideas need to be replaced. One of the most difficult parts of a church doing needs-based evangelism is simply managing the mission. When laity is given permission to reach out, they will. There is no magic formula for this kind of management. It requires involvement, good communication, and a clear system of coordination of every activity, a strong financial management strategy by the laity of the church, and an entrepreneurial understanding by the pastor and key leaders.

In order for the entrepreneurial, needs-based, permission-giving church to function, there must be a system of putting ministry committees and task groups in operation. The local church needs to develop a system that is quick and effective, a system of coordinating that does not allow groups to run into one another, a system that manages the flow of program and money, a system that is responsible and still evangelistic. Often, the Finance Committee has the task of seeing that the enthusiasm for meeting needs does not outrun the financial resources to support this enthusiasm. This is always a difficult, yet important task.

Quality

The final organizational characteristic of needs-based church is quality. One of the clearest twenty-first-century needs is quality. Because we are so competitive, people will not tolerate dirty bathrooms, inefficient nursery staff, fumbling ushers, and poor quality music. One of the harder aspects of a needs-based congregation is to see that it is done correctly. In a volunteer organization, it is always difficult to have quality in every aspect of the church. However, the church must have that as its basic goal: to do things well.

A congregation's compassionate leaders who are caring must be intolerant of ineffective, poorly managed ministries. The goal is too great to let it be bungled. Consequently, churches need to choose their ministries carefully. Most churches do not have the resources to do extensive ministries. They need to choose the ministries that they have the ability to do well, the energy to follow up on, and the passion to invite other people to be involved.

Change Stinking Thinking

I was in a conversation that involved several friends who were a part of the recovery program. They had gone through some tough times in their lives. All three had become active in the Alcoholics Anonymous program. They had become leaders in the twelve-step process and now were part of a church-based recovery program using the twelve steps. We were discussing dysfunctional living habits and problems of substance abuse.

One of these individuals continually used the phrase "stinking thinking." I know in recovery meetings, that phrase is sometimes used. To me, it really communicated that a lot of us just have bad thinking. We haven't gotten the answer figured out well. We are trying to succeed but are stuck in dysfunctional and ineffective ways of thinking things out. We suffer. The leaders of local mainline churches across America, as well as many of the participants, suffer from "stinking thinking."

Some of those dysfunctional ways of thinking about things are to allow our motivation, plans, and vocational lives to be driven by professional thinking, rather than by missional thinking. We make decisions about things considering: will it advance us professionally? Will I get a promotion? Will we get a bigger church? Will we please our District Superintendent? We make decisions on an institutional basis, rather than on a missional basis. Our direction is inward, involving the maze of relationships, reward systems, punishment systems, and culture that is our denomination, local church, and group of churches. We have neglected being concerned about what is the true meaning and purpose of the church, that is, making disciples; and the real goal, too often, seems to be making advancement in our careers.

Another form of ineffective thinking is to separate the evangelistic thrust of the church from the social sensitivity or the social justice thrust of the church. Today, denominations are split. We label people by their vocabulary. Clergy talk about working for social justices and tell stories about the AIDS crisis in Africa and the lack of women's rights in America. The stories in these conversations indicate which side of the church theological issues we are on. Others speak about winning people for Christ, seeker-sensitive worship, concern about abortion, and the lack of biblical authority. Again, the approach is to divide two central parts of the Christian faith. Meeting needs and leading people to Christ are the same thing. They function together, such as speaking and hearing. They are part of the same system.

In Luke 4, Jesus did not separate his concern for people with his concern for salvation in any way. In James' writings, the concepts are tied together clearly. He states in James 2:14, "What good is it, my brothers and sisters, if you say you have faith but do not have works? Can faith save you?" Paul's discussion of the church in numerous places combines meeting the needs of the people with the proclamation of the authentic gospel. Read Romans 12. First John 4:20 says, "Those who say, 'I love God,' and hate their brothers or sisters are liars." Love of God and others is the same. We must understand that true evangelism will happen when we relate to the real needs of people around us and around the world.

The concept of limiting the possibilities of what a church can do is one of the most "stinking thinking" practices of Christians. The growing, entrepreneurial churches, such as Lakewood Church or Saddleback or Fellowship Church in Grapevine, Texas, have been built upon doing the impossible. Mike Slaughter became pastor of a small rural-type suburban church. Who would have thought that that church could become one of the mega-churches of our society? It seems impossible that a congregation at Ginghamsburg, Ohio, would become a leader in digital, visual, and experiential worship. The congregation has continued to grow. When we limit ourselves, limit the vision, limit the dream, and limit the hope, we limit the power of the gospel to use the church to reach new people for Christ.

CHAPTER 7

NICHE MARKETING AND NEEDS

A Simple Idea

Instructions for the life of the church and the life of a Christian are to make disciples of Jesus Christ and to help other people be like the evangelists on the day of Pentecost and like the good Samaritan, found in Luke 10. Caring for human need, dealing with social justice, and leading people to Jesus Christ are not contraries, but they are part of the same presentation. When needs are met, people find the experience of God in their lives, and they want to be part of a caring, life-changing church.

The methodology, then, of reaching people for Christ is to be like the good Samaritan. The strategy for being a good Samaritan church might be described in secular ways as niche marketing—that is, responding to a specific need and offering answers and solutions to that need. Needs-based evangelism is based upon good Samaritan theology, the Great Commission, and an understanding that we must choose what needs we can seek to meet. Those doing marketing would describe this as "niche marketing." It is not some manipulative style of advertising or sale; it's simply common sense. Market, or evangelize, in the areas where there is a need or an openness. Evangelize where you are strong and where you can meet that need and share the gospel well.

Niche marketing is a term developed by secular advertising and salespeople as a way to help industry target their efforts. Niche marketing is based upon finding the aspects of society in which the products and services that you have are needed and no one, or few, are offering answers. Niche marketing is based upon good research of the culture, a clear understanding of the product, and definite strategy to make the product available to the individuals of society who need it most. It's also based upon understanding and evaluation of others that are seeking to meet the need and not trying to compete where the need is already being met. Seek to offer your product or services in a niche where there is not only a need, but also where few are answering the need. This concept can help the church reach its target to be like the good Samaritan—to care in the way that is most effective and to respond in way in which the church has the best resources. The reality is that when we meet needs, people want to be a part of our church. When we meet needs and present the gospel at the same time, they will be responsive, see the gospel in action, and, potentially, will join the Christian community to be a part of those disciples of Jesus Christ.

Meeting Needs

Bethany was the new pastor of a young congregation at the edge of a metropolitan area. She was the second pastor—the first pastor had gotten the church started and then made some serious mistakes and had to move all too soon. She was there to heal, help, and start the church all over again. She visited the pastor of the church where she had grown up and shared her situation. She talked to two of her seminary classmates and shared the situation. She met with the district superintendent and asked questions. She wanted to know what to do. In every case, she wasn't quite satisfied with the answer. You see, she felt the imperative of the social justice issues that some of her seminary professors had helped her see. She was concerned about the environment, the needs of the poor, and AIDS in Africa. Her more evangelical friends had raised serious questions concerning the importance of leading people to Christ and the imperative to follow the Great Commission. She prayed and studied and prayed and studied, asking what should the goals and directions of this new church be. Certainly the answer had to do with the people who were already members. Certainly the answer had to do with the community in which the church was, and certainly the answer had to do with what skills she had in leadership, but she needed a strategy. Bethany was like all of us; she needed a strategy, a mission, a purpose, an imperative.

The United Methodist Church stated several years ago that our mission purpose strategy was to "make disciples of Jesus Christ." In the midst of our diversity, we came up with a single-sentence answer. But how do you do that? In a highly secular, very consumer-driven society, how do you make disciples? Charles Sheldon, answering this question in 1896, would have said you do it by simply asking *What would Jesus do?* It was too simple for sophisticated theologians, and yet that is the very point. It is simple. Jesus described his ministry as meeting needs and called us to do the same. Jesus commissioned his followers to make disciples and that's it.

As I came to be pastor of Christ United Methodist Church in Tulsa in 1969, the church was going through a difficult transition: finances were bad and membership had declined significantly. In the midst of that, the simple ideas of Charles Sheldon in asking, *What would Jesus do?* seemed to be a powerful answer to our struggle. Charles Sheldon's novel, *In His Steps*, that became a Christian best-seller, puts it simply. He taught to build the life of a church upon a theology of action, of behavior. We called it the "Christyle," combining the two words "Christ" and "style" together in describing who we are. In doing that, the Great Commandment and the Great Commission became key for defining a church concerned with helping others and leading people to become followers of Jesus Christ.

So what is the strategy? Marketing experts might call it niche marketing. First, we begin with an understanding of the needs. Second, we seek an understanding of our resources. Third, the church sets priorities. Fourth, the church develops a plan to mobilize. Fifth, clergy and key leaders begin the program of meeting needs, sharing the gospel, and helping people become involved in God's church. In Luke 4, Jesus said the needs were to bring "good news," free the captives, help the blind see, and let the oppressed go free. That was the task in the first century. In the twenty-first century, the task may have to do with family problems, world hunger, justice for minorities, chronic depression, divorce, vocational change, and basic spirituality. When needs are met, faith can be shared and people will come to Christ. Meeting social human needs and evangelism go together!

Categories of Needs

Needs or niches can be divided into a whole series of different categories: needs that have to do with generations, from the boomers to the millennials; needs that have to do with transition times, from retirement to college graduation; needs that have to do with major social issues, drugs, divorce, hunger, and poverty; needs that have to do with personal growth, relationship skills, purpose in life, and self-esteem. Other groupings of people and needs may have to do with place in life or times of transition. Needs may have to do with social issues, questions of justice, or missional concern. All these provide arenas for the church to set its mission and purpose.

In setting the categories of needs, our church felt that a major need had to do with families. The question was, "How do you help families?" For us at Christ Church, the answer was to start a counseling center. Starting with one Christian counselor, eventually with eight full-time therapists, we sought to meet a variety of categories of needs that had to do with personal problems, family problems, and vocational problems. People came to counseling and came to church.

In a totally different way, often, people seeking ways to be healthier have good exercise with other Christians and take part in organized recreational and fitness activities. We've had a bicycling club, a jogging club, aerobics classes, walking groups—all seeking to meet a need, and all helping people become a part of the church fellowship.

Niche Marketing and the Church's Mission

Niche marketing is a secular way of speaking about finding a specific need and meeting it. The church is called to be like the good Samaritan and to respond to needs, and the church is called to be like Jesus as he described his mission in Luke 4. The church, in following the steps of Jesus, must respond to the hurts and needs of individuals and groups of individuals of the culture. As we respond to the need, or the niche, in our society where we perceive a need, if we are intentional, the gospel of Jesus Christ will be shared. If you are invitational and invite those who come for help to participate in the ultimate help, or the love of God, then evangelism and social concerns become the same thing.

In Tulsa, several years ago, needs within the Native American community were not being met. Our church made a decision to get involved directly in supporting the interests of Native Americans in Tulsa to build a Native American United Methodist community center. The community center was developed in cooperation with other Native American United Methodist programs, and out of it, some people came to the church and became active because they were helped by the ministry, and others came because they wanted to be in a church where they could help the Native American community.

The needs vary from issues of generations, lifestyles, personal problems, crises, marriage, divorce, family life, children, youth, retirement, and death. The list goes on and on. The needs are spiritual, physical, relational, social, and personal.

Most of the growing churches across America can define their growth in terms of their ability to meet the real needs of persons in our society. In 1994, a group of members in our congregation saw the need for developing contemporary worship. With the help of Vern, Delia, and Leanne, one of the finest pioneering contemporary worship services in our denomination was developed. Because we were able to meet the needs of people who enjoyed contemporary music, who found a refreshing power in that music, and who wanted the creativity offered in a contemporary worship service, the church doubled in size in the 1990s. A whole new part of the Tulsa community became involved in that contemporary worship—mostly baby boomers and Gen Xers. They were captured by the music and the creativity, needs were being met, and commitments to Jesus Christ were being made.

He was known as a marketing guy. Everybody in the church knew that Bill was a salesman. He had been a salesman all his life. His college degree was in marketing and business management. He knew the vocabulary. He was director for marketing and sales for the small manufacturing company that he worked for. He was known in his manufacturing field as the key guru on sales. So when any individual in the church or any of his friends needed a little advice on marketing and sales, Bill was the guy, and he liked to give advice.

He had the theories down pat. So when the discussion in the church council meeting focused upon buying new equipment for the children's playground, Bill sat and listened to the arguments. Can we afford it? Should it be done? Was it worth it for the limited amount of use? It was like the whole discussion was shaking him up like a bottle of cola with the lid on. Finally it was more than he could stand and he "popped his cork." With emotion, he began to sell.

He said, "The question about children's equipment is not a question about how often the equipment will be used, but will it help us to reach more young couples and families? Our decision is a niche marketing decision. Do we want to put our emphasis upon marketing to families and their children or upon youth? Should the niche that our church serves be one mostly for retired people? Or should it be for the poor or for the rich? We are a medium-sized church. We can't do everything for everybody. So, we need to decide.

"You are trying to decide about a playground. The real question is, is it a priority that we reach children? If it is, the playground is a pretty good way. Everybody who drives by the church will see the new playground. Kids will love it. Parents will like to leave their children at the church. It's good advertising."

He went on to say, "If our major goal is to reach the elderly, maybe the playground is not so important. Most of us are over sixty-five. We are not interested at all in noisy children, playgrounds, or anything that has to do with it. To build a playground is counterproductive for us. We want people who are like us. We have a great Friday night bridge group. We need some more players. Our senior citizen Sunday school class is one of the best in town. We need some more people. We are starting a senior's choir. A lot of us enjoy it. We don't need a bunch of little kids around."

So he concluded by saying, "You have to decide what niche God is calling you to serve." He paused for a moment and said, "Maybe you can do two niches, maybe even three, but God's only given us so many resources and so much money, so let's be smart." It was quiet in the room when he finished.

Someone said, "Bill, it kind of sounds like you are saying birds of a feather flock together and that we ought to do what we do best." Bill said, "Well that's not what I said. But it's the truth. Choose your market areas. Choose one that you are strong in, and people will come. People will respond positively to being with people they know and like, and they will grow as followers of Jesus."

Don't Separate the Help from the Love

One of the tragedies of Christians today is that so often we provide help but never tell about the love of God. We give food to the homeless and never share with them the joy and the personal growth that comes from knowing the power of God in our lives. We offer a senior citizens program and provide exercise classes for the aging, and yet we never give them an invitation or opportunity to be a part of Sunday school classes and prayer groups and worship services. We have become apologetic about evangelism, and, consequently, our care is superficial and, in most cases, is seen as hypocritical. When people do not respect those who are helping, they show that disrespect in their rejection of the ideas and institutions of those who help. Helping is an opportunity to show love.

In most mainline local churches, one area in which this mistake is made most often is in weekday preschool childcare or daycare during which a church offers ministry to children, but does it in a secular way. It is tragic that churches all across America have strong preschool education or childcare but never enthusiastically share the gospel. The effect is that the parents of the preschoolers in the end do not respect the church, because the church has not upheld its authenticity. Goals for preschool education need to be, of course, quality care and education, but also a clear presentation of the gospel of Jesus Christ to children and particularly to their parents in times of transition, such as divorce, family crisis, loss of job, and so on. When help and evangelism are brought together, love and care become one and the same, and people come to know Christ through the caring ministries of the church.

How Does It Work?

When we seek to respond to those needs, people are affected for Christ in two ways. First, when the need is met in an individual's life, he or she can see Christ in the meeting of the need. That individual wants to be a part of a fellowship of love. When needs are met for the individual, typically, he or she is in a time of transition, which means that he or she is in a time of evaluation, processing, re-examination, and searching. It is at those moments that we are most likely to be open to the gospel of Jesus Christ and the message that Christ has brought.

He was a resident in the halfway house that our denomination had developed. We were his sponsor and actively involved in this criminal justice ministry. He not only received the help of the church, but also became an active participant in the life of the church. When needs are met, people become a part of the family of God.

The second way in which needs-based evangelism works is out of the authenticity of being a church meeting needs. Many people are searching for a good church, an authentic church, a nonmanipulative church, a welcoming church, a caring church, a friendly church. When the church is doing what God wants us to do, people want to be a part of that church that is helping! For many people, the gospel is proclaimed when they see the authentic representation of the message of Jesus. They become disciples when they become a part of a truly loving church.

In the 1990s, some churches in America became excited about the possibility of going to Russia and helping start new churches after the fall of communism. In our church, we found that people wanted to be a part of a church helping start churches in Russia. They saw this as authentic, not fake, and they made a decision about their faith in terms of being members of our church because of our mission. A large church in Minneapolis very much involved in AIDS ministry attracted many new members because they wanted to be part of a church that was dealing with a significant social issue of today's society. In Tulsa, where racial problems have been a significant issue, two predominantly African American churches and Christ Church, which is predominantly non–African American, began to have worship services together. People came to the church because of the Unity Services. They wanted to take a stand for the issue of social justice; and when the church was meeting that need, they wanted to be a part of that kind of church.

The opportunities for needs-based evangelism are unlimited. The only limits are our imagination, sensitivity, organizational skills, and clarity of witness.

In the next few chapters, we'll see some descriptions of areas of needs-based evangelism, niches where the church can meet needs and witness to the gospel in a powerful way. We'll review some high-profile needs, such as singles ministry and personal growth, and we'll review how one can witness in the midst of meeting those needs. The possibilities are unlimited because God's love frees us for joyful obedience.

CHAPTER 8

SINGLES MINISTRY AND EVANGELISM

Our Greatest Need?

There is no need more devastating than the need of an individual who is experiencing divorce. The percentage of marriages coming apart in American society varies by community. We can generalize by recognizing that as many as one-half of marriages will end in divorce. This means that a major part of American society will experience this trauma. Divorce devastates both individuals, disrupts lives of children, and sets a ripple effect through family and friends. Divorce forces a reordering of many relationships. It deals with issues of self-esteem, guilt, anger, resentment, abuse, rebuilding, establishing goals, vocational transition, moving, dating, planning, depression, excitement, hurt, and a desperate need for a spiritual relationship with God.

Churches across American have found it difficult to deal with this great need. Normal programming for churches is family oriented, and couples oriented. Because divorce involves so much—such a high level of feeling, such complexity of relationships—churches tend to neglect or simply ignore families and individuals going through divorce. Because we want and desire to affirm the sanctity of marriage and the importance of the marriage vows, it becomes difficult for churches to deal with situations in which marriages are coming apart and commitments are breaking.

Mainline Protestant churches stand in an unusual place to minister to those going through divorce because that part of the American Christian community that most often uses guilt, judgment, and fear as a part of their means of communicating within the congregation can offer nothing else to these hurting people. So often people going through divorce find in those churches only condemnation and judgment and experience guilt, resentment, and anger. Oftentimes, deeply committed Christians whose marriages come apart find that they are doubly condemned, not only by the failure of the marriage, but also by the judgment and the guilt that is poured out on them by their own congregation. Usually, people who are a part of dysfunctional marriages quit attending churches that operate on guilt and fear because it is so painful. Mainline Protestant churches that focus more on God's grace rather than God's judgment find themselves in an unusual, advantageous position to minister to individuals going through divorce.

Divorce Ministry

Of all the needs that can be met by the mainline Protestant church, one that it is most equipped to meet is the need of divorce. The tools of support, love, care, therapy, training, and rebuilding are programs and procedures that most mainline Protestant churches already have in place or have ready resources to put into place. Because this transition is so traumatic, it provides an opportunity to share the gospel in a way that is available in few other ministry settings. Persons going through divorce want to hear about the love of God through Jesus Christ. They are desperate to know that God loves them and cares for them in the midst of their hurt. The message of Christ's atoning sacrifice for our sins is a means by which people who feel the guilt can know the forgiveness.

Allison was thirty-five years old, had been married for seven years, and had two children. Her husband had an affair with his coworker. Allison and her husband had gone to counseling and reconciled. Then there was another affair. There was anger, some abuse, lots of dysfunctional family experiences; and the marriage came apart. They had gone to church earlier in their marriage, and yet, when things began to get bad, they quit going. Her family was helping. Friends were supportive. Yet, she was so angry she cried herself to sleep most nights, and it seemed to her that nobody understood. She was a typical single parent, back to work in the vocation she had been trained for before she got married, with two kids in daycare, parents helping when they could, but not enough money. She was angry, depressed, and unsure. Allison's best friend told her about a divorce adjustment workshop at a church. She had heard of the singles program at the church and did not really feel like she was single, even though she was. But she was desperate, so she went to the workshop.

The workshop was built upon a simple idea of spending two days together in small groups discussing issues of divorce and recovery. All the leaders had gone through divorce themselves. The talks were from a Christian perspective but were mostly practical advice about decision-making, self-esteem, and the basic building blocks for rebuilding your life. She became acquainted with the team leaders who were all a part of the church. She was invited to the singles Sunday school group the next Sunday. She was invited to activities during the week, almost every night. People in the weekend workshop were organizing a support group.

After the weekend workshop, she felt totally different. After four weeks, she was well into the process of rebuilding. She was functioning well; her children were in Sunday school, and they were all involved in the life of the church. She looked for ways that she could do leadership in the church, herself. She said, "This church saved my life." On the Sunday that she joined the church and was baptized, she was surrounded by her new friends and she was affirmed!

I have found that of the people who come to Christ Church in Tulsa for our divorce adjustment program, one-half to two-thirds are not involved in any church, and half of them never made a commitment of their lives to Christ. I have found that half the people who come and get involved in the church divorce ministry become involved in the church within three months, make a commitment to Christ, and join the church. Most of them have not been active in a church. The ministry to people going through divorce is powerfully effective. It is what Jesus would do, and the divorced people who are part of the program make a commitment to become involved in God's church and find peace and power that they need.

Christians who have gone through divorce must operate divorce ministry. It must be built upon a concept of grace. It must involve peer ministry, that is, people helping one another. It cannot be a quick fix model, but it must be built upon a process, a community of love and support, lots of training in the building blocks of recovery and time. A church that believes in helping people who hurt must surround divorce ministry. It must be built with a support program of singles activities that are helpful and exciting.

Support of the Congregation

It is an imperative for a successful singles program that there is general congregational support for ministry to single people. This is true of any kind of needs-based evangelism. Whether the congregation is seeking to minister to singles, young couples, retirees, the unemployed, AIDS victims, leukemia families, or others, the congregation needs to have a clear commitment to the area of ministry. This usually means that key leaders within the congregation have a passion for that area. There will be criticism and discomfort by the congregation in dealing with people who have a defined set of needs. There will be criticism of any congregation spending too much time helping the cancer support group, the teenagers, and the old people, whatever the ministry is. Consequently, there must be clear structural support within the congregation for the ministry, continual positive publicity about the ministry, and an unwavering belief that this is what Jesus would do, that is, a theological commitment to helping people in need.

Local Church Based

Ministry has to be clearly local church based. It will not work effectively if it is ecumenical, shared by a judicatory, or done jointly with several churches. The basic unit for Christian ministry is the local church. The local church has support, care, organizational function, financial stability, and most of all, a community in which discipleship can be done. Any time a singles ministry or any particular needs-based evangelism is done with a multiple local church focus, what is everyone's responsibility ends up being no one's responsibility. People take advantage of the help, but without a local congregation highly involved, they do not become involved in the church, make their commitment to Jesus Christ, and become disciples. Do not do singles ministry ecumenically or cooperatively. This is not because of some arrogant sense of the local church's place in the community. It is simply a practical understanding of what works.

Widows and Widowers

Ministry to widows and widowers can be one of the most satisfying areas of ministry within the broader area of singles ministry. Widows and widowers suffer the same devastation as people going through divorce. The difference is they do not have the same anger, hurt, and devastation to self-esteem that happens in divorce. There is anger, hurt, and problems of self-esteem, but it is expressed differently. Widows and widowers ministry can be done in cooperation with other singles ministry, but it must have a separate identity. They need to have their own support group, their own support system, their own network of relationships, and their own focus of ministry. It is a serious mistake to assume that widows, widowers, and divorced persons will function together. They can sometimes, but not all the time.

Martha's husband died of cancer two years ago. The hurt and the loneliness had been devastating, yet she simply did not want to get out with groups of people. She stayed home a lot. Her kids were deeply concerned.

Ed's wife died in a car wreck. They were going on a vacation together in the first few months of his retirement. He simply was broken-hearted. He did not know what to do with retirement and the death of his spouse at the same time. Ed searched for all kinds of answers. He went to therapy and even signed up for a dating service.

Ed and Martha both saw the newspaper ad about the workshop for people who had lost a spouse through death. They both showed up in the same workshop. They were in the same small group. They shared. They told their stories and shared their feelings and frustrations. They were ministered to by the other widows and widowers in the group, and they started coming to the widow and widower support group. After support group, the group generally went out for coffee and pie at a local restaurant. Ed and Martha were a part of that large group. But as the weeks went on, there seemed to be an attraction. They got involved in the church. Ironically, they both joined the church on the same Sunday. Ed had not been to church for years, and he felt it strange that he was back in church after being away since he was a teenager. But he felt good about it. After a year and a half of being involved in the support group, Ed and Martha started dating, just informally. They knew that what happened to them was part of God's healing plan. On the day of their wedding, the sanctuary was filled with 150 members of the widow and widower support group celebrating healing and hope.

Singles Program

Successful singles activities involve fellowship, spiritual growth, strong church relationship, activities to help singles develop relationships, classes on personal growth and development and relationships, service projects on behalf of the local church and community, a strong enthusiastic support from the senior pastor, congregational leadership, congregation in general and other staff, and a focus on the priority of singles ministry.

Singles ministries can vary from ministry with young singles just out of college, ministry with those in their late twenties and thirties, ministry for never-marrieds, ministry for widows and widowers, or a ministry built upon divorce care. Because the needs of single people are so varied, it is difficult for a local church to do more than one of these areas.

Christ United Methodist Church in Tulsa has one of the largest singles groups in any denomination in the country, ministering to five hundred to fifteen hundred persons.

The primary focus of this ministry is on divorced persons. The secondary focus is on ministry to widows and widowers.

We have found that successful singles ministry involves activities almost every night of the week and lots of activities on the weekend. Activities provide a means to social-ize and reestablish friends and build new relationships. Activities can vary from dances to meetings about personal growth, from prayer groups to support groups. Activities need to be highly publicized and communicated clearly and often so that people can easily find out what is going on. Singles ministry functions best if it is directed by the participants, that is, staff can help and coach, but there needs to be organization from within the singles community so that the singles program belongs to the participants. The organization of the singles program needs to be a part of the regular church func-tioning, not separate from the church, but under the basic organization of any local church under the authority of that local church. Leadership, committee members, and so on should be loyal, active members of the church. Unless the connection with local churches maintains authority, singles ministry tends, naturally, to become more and more secular. The local church should insist that all leaders are committed members of the church. All leadership is approved in the normal nominating process, and pro-grams and activities are approved in the normal decision-making process of the church. Any sense of separation or different treatment becomes extremely dysfunctional for the effectiveness of the singles program.

Summary

Singles is one of the most powerful, clear, Christ-inspired ministries that a local church can do today. It is desperately needed. It is one of the clearest means of evan-gelism available today. If the mainline Protestant churches would enthusiastically embrace singles ministry, churches would grow significantly. The vitality of the con-gregation would change.

The beautiful thing about needs-based evangelism is that when a church meets the needs of those who are hurting, the hurting person understands from the beginning what needs-based evangelism is and that they want to be leaders and participants in future needs-based evangelistic activities. The joy of singles ministry, based upon divorce ministry or widow and widower ministry, is that when people go through the process and find healing and hope, they want to share it. In fact, you can't stop them from sharing it.

CHAPTER 9

OUR PERSONAL NEEDS

The Scope of Personal Needs

One of the most basic ways Jesus Christ helps hurting people to touch their spiritual lives. The Bible is filled with stories of healing, of helping with relationships, of giving a sense of purpose, of dealing with human self-esteem, and of ministering to deep spiritual longings. The church is called to meet those needs whether or not they are involved in church. Meeting personal needs is a major area of the good Samaritan church's life, whether it's helping persons with their purpose in life, vocational changes, relationships, self-esteem, recovery, spiritual life, or counseling needs; the church is called to be there to help and to lead people to the way of Christ.

Purpose in Life and Meeting Needs

I wandered with my family to a large discount mega-store. Things were stacked to the ceiling and bargains were everywhere. As part of the consumer generation, we were there to shop, to be part of the culture, and to find a good deal. And then I saw it, a giant stack of books. As a clergyperson it was hard to believe. There were more books in that stack than in any other down that long full aisle of books. The marvelous thing about the stack of books was that the book was written by a clergyperson. A Southern Baptist preacher from California wrote a best seller. He wrote a book that everybody needed and everybody wanted. Christians and non-Christians alike purchased Rick Warren's *The Purpose-Driven Life*. Churches of all denominations and sizes have organized study groups, support groups, and preaching series on the book because purpose in life is a basic need.

Long before Rick Warren, Victor Frankl and Abraham Maslow preached the priority of purpose. Frankl developed a therapy called logo therapy around the idea that one of the basic needs of every human being was meaning.

If we are to reach people for Jesus Christ, we must meet the heart of their personal needs whether the needs are found in the preaching schedules suggested in the liturgical year or not. If we do not meet needs in preaching, people do not come. Niche marketing or needs-based evangelism is built upon touching the life of the individual where the individual needs help. One of those most pressing needs is a sense of purpose.

We all need meaning and purpose. The gospel grants the answer to our need. Meeting the needs of meaning and purpose is one of the most powerful ways to reach new people for Jesus Christ.

Vocational Change

In the highly technological world in which we live, with continual change both cultural and technological, people are making vocational changes, vocational changes that cause economic success or failure. Vocational changes can mean moving from one city to another. Most individuals today change vocations five or six times in their life. Most companies reorganize over and over. Consequently, meeting the needs brought about by vocational change is a way to help people with one of the greatest crises they face and to show them the answers that Christ's message brings to people dealing with vocational transition: what it means to be a child of God, how the gospel helps us in using our resources, and understanding our direction in life are key questions every person has. The church, if we want to help people be disciples of Jesus Christ, must be the best vocational training place in town.

Jason was thirty-six. He had held three different jobs since he graduated from college. When the last company he worked for reorganized, he was let go. He had been job searching for three months when his best friend told him about a workshop that was being held at a local church. The workshop was for people out of work. It gave job-hunting training. The group was a kind of support group. They met twice a week and had prayer. Someone provided information about the job market. Someone else gave a lesson about how to hunt for work. Others discussed issues of depression and frustration during the job search. The first night he went, he felt better. He began to go regularly. He joined the group that met at the church every morning in the chapel for prayer before they went out to make contacts. The church had a room with computers and telephones that could be used. Lots of days, he simply went to that room so he could be with the others who were searching, too. He and his wife were inactive members of a local church, but now he found himself at church almost every day. It was normal that the family started attending worship. He had made so many friends in the job search group that being in church was just continuing to be with those friends. The church had a place where church members who knew of job openings could list those jobs. Eventually, he found the employment he was looking for. There was a counselor who worked with the job support group who offered him some great advice and help. In the course of the job search, Jason and his family became active in the church. He said for the first time in his life, he really committed himself to Jesus Christ as Lord and Savior. He's now the leader of the job support group. Not only is he offering ministry and help, but also he's one of the biggest evangelists for the church through the job support group.

Relationships

Marriages are in trouble, divorce is up, there is conflict in the workplace as well as in the world, children don't get along together, and people have few friends. These are characteristics of our modern life. Visit the self-help section of any bookstore and you will find the aisles are packed full of coaching on how to have better relationships. It's not just how to win friends, but it's also how to get along, talk, communicate, relate, show affection, manage business, organize people, and sell products. It all deals with relationships. Jesus taught us how to get along together. Paul's best advice is found in the love chapter, 1 Corinthians 13. Jesus' Sermon on the Mount is about relationships. Churches that want to grow need to have classes on marriage, parenting, communications, conflict management, and love languages. If we want to reach people, we need to be relevant, and the most relevant topic today is relationships.

Churches can provide relationship training as a part of their regular church school or Sunday school. Curriculum can be bought, developed, or built and will provide opportunities for people to build better relationships. Weeknight study groups and workshops can be organized to help people develop relationship skills. There are excellent therapists and counselors who provide Christian material on relationships. These books and materials can be made available at the church. Preaching and worship needs to deal with relationships with others as well as with relationships with God. Good preaching should provide reference to the resources for developing better skills and relationships. Sermon illustrations can motivate people to get help as stories are told about those who grow in their ability to love their neighbor as themselves. The Bible makes it clear that our business is love. We need lots of love training offered through the church.

Self-Esteem

There are seven things not to do in the four middle verses of the love chapter in Corinthians. All seven of those things destroy self-esteem. Being arrogant, rude, jealous, boastful, irritable, resentful, and insisting on our own way all clobber self-esteem. Most educators and child psychologists agree that unless we have appropriately strong self-esteem, we will not grow up to be healthy. Most counselors dealing with marriage conflict or dysfunctional relationships often see self-esteem problems by one or more of the people involved. Paul tells us that God is for us. Paul reminds us in Romans 8 that nothing can separate us from the love of Jesus Christ. God obviously wants us to love ourselves, not in a selfish or inordinately prideful way, but in a way that helps us have the courage and stamina to reach out to love others.

If we are to practice needs-based evangelism or niche marketing, we need to present our greatest product, which is unquestionable self-esteem. Paul says, "We are more than conquerors through him who loved us" (Romans 8:37) and "I can do all things through him who strengthens me" (Philippians 4:13). He tells us to put on the armor of God to fight off the fiery darts of the devil. Churches that want to grow must cultivate the self-esteem of the congregation, bringing this message of God's amazing love to people who are desperate to know that they are loved, that they are important and that their life counts. One of the strongest things a local church can do to reach more people is to see that the preaching, teaching, and the areas of ministry deal with building self-esteem. From the way we treat babies in the nursery to the way we conduct funerals, affirmation, love, and healthy self-esteem are standards. When this is done, people's basic needs are met and they will want to be followers of Jesus.

Allen and Mary Beth had not been to church in years. Their parents didn't attend church; they visited a few times when they were teenagers. Now that they had two young children of their own, they had needs and were desperate. In their neighborhood, there were no young kids, and no young families. The kids were bored. Their third-grader was bashful and had a learning problem. Their children needed friends. As parents in a secular culture, they were worried about values, morals, and their kids. When their good friends invited them to attend church with them they were reluctant, fearful, a little confused, and yet they were willing to try it. When their children came home and said they loved Sunday school, when they got a personal letter from the teacher of their five-year-old daughter, and when their third-grader received a phone call from her Sunday school teacher speaking to her about the plans for next Sunday, they knew that they had found an answer to desperate needs. They visited the classrooms and found they were bright, cheerful, creative, and magnificent in the techniques they used in teaching and multisensory learning. They realized this was not a place of boredom and guilt and fear, but a place of joy and growth and affirmation. These two very secular parents became enthusiastic followers of Jesus just because the church they visited believed and taught God's love clearly!

Recovery

Recovery ministry is needed in every community. The problems of substance abuse, addictions, and dysfunctional personalities are common. We hear the news stories of lives out of control and are horrified; and yet in every family, all across our nation, there are abuses, addictions, phobias, and fears that could describe our whole culture as sick. Whether alcohol abuse, sexual abuse, or other compulsive behavior, the church can be there to provide help, love, and direction. The love of Jesus Christ meets us at every point of need and certainly at this most complex and hurtful point.

Recovery programs have become some of the most successful means to reach new people. A Friday night worship service, support groups, and training can be a way in which a whole new part of the community can find themselves a church. Sometimes recovery programs need to be somewhat segregated from the mainstream of the church simply because of anonymity. Other times these programs can be mainstreamed into the life of the church. In either case, they provide powerful ways to help a hurting world and effective ways to bring people to the way of Jesus and help them become devoted followers of Jesus Christ. The list of areas of recovery is endless.

Methods of Meeting Personal Growth Needs

The methodologies of ministry of personal growth vary from classes to preaching. Personal growth can become a part of a choir Christmas program or an Easter sunrise service. Personal growth can be a focus of Sunday school curriculum for adults, children, and youth. Some of the mega-churches in our country have built themselves upon providing general personal growth help. From the preaching to the classes and workshops offered under Dr. Robert Schuller's ministry, the focus was on personal growth and help. Kirbyjon Caldwell built the largest church in Methodism, Windsor Village United Methodist Church, by meeting personal growth needs in very direct and clear ways. Earl Paulk at Cathedral at Chapel Hill in Atlanta has combined strong worship ministries with ministries that relate directly and powerfully to the personal needs of the people in the community.

Spiritual Needs

Surveys that have been made of the American population over the last ten years, whether that population is rural or urban, red states or blue states, show the same basic need. In a secular world, it is surprising to find what usually comes to the top of the survey. Most Americans responding to a survey's questions about their primary needs speak about spiritual needs. This is not necessarily defined as a religious need or church attendance, but it is expressed with deep concern and longing. People today have a longing for the spiritual. There are countless ways this is expressed. All kinds of groups, books, and activities seek to meet this longing for the spiritual. Obviously, the church has the corner on this part of the market. The problem is, because of our determination to see that spiritual needs are met in a specific denominational or theological way, we often miss the opportunity actually to meet those needs. Using a variety of music and worship styles, techniques of prayer and preaching, visual imaging, and metaphor help people find the answer to their spiritual needs.

With spiritual needs being at the top of most people's list, it should provide for the church the biggest opportunity to lead people to Jesus Christ. We must find what it is within our systems of belief and church life that turns people off and chase them away from the very source of the answer to their basic need. We long for God. Paul says our spirits cry out to God's spirit. It is the way we are made. In the church needs-based evangelism program, we must offer a variety of ways to meet spiritual longing. Church leaders and clergy need to be open to experimentation and, at the same time, clear about the authentic values of our faith.

A large church in a northern urban city held worship services in a community building in the older section of town built in the 1920s and 1930s. The services are creative. They involve everything from contemporary worship, contemporary music, the sacrament of Holy Communion, and the labyrinth. The services vary from quiet candlelight to loud music. In the midst of those experimental services, literally hundreds of younger Americans come to God.

Support and Counseling

Meeting personal needs can be done through a multitude of means—organizing support groups and providing counseling both help. Churches that care about people will find the many ways to help people grow. Needs-based evangelism, when it focuses on the personal needs, can be a part of almost everything a church does, reaching every generation in unlimited ways.

Churches can provide effective help by developing counseling programs that can be done within the church, sponsored, operated, and supervised by the church; or the church may provide a facility where local Christian counselors can rent space. Oftentimes, a partnership, for example, can be helpful so counselors can provide workshops and training, as well as therapeutic counseling support.

In the façade of American culture, we often think that everything is great and there are no difficulties. Everyone is healthy. Families are functional, and life is smooth and sweet. Yet, with all the prosperity and the possibilities of American society, there are many needs and places where people are hurting. It is at those places that the church can bring the gospel of Jesus Christ to bring healing and new life. When the church responds to the personal needs of individuals, we bring the gospel at a point of openness to learn, to listen, and to become followers of Jesus Christ. Needs represent the opportunity to share and the opportunity for people to be open to accept and follow Christ.

Churches all across America have organized a variety of support groups and counseling. Oftentimes, support groups center around areas of health needs. Cancer support groups are among those support groups that provide much-needed optimistic, hopeful, and loving support.

Billie lost her husband to a heart problem, and then found out she had cancer. Devastated in every way, it was the cancer support group at the church that gave her a sense of peace—not only the peace to deal with her own cancer and to conquer it, but also the opportunity eventually to lead the cancer support group in helping others and leading them to the way of Christ.

Helping and Hope

In meeting personal needs, the church offers the greatest gift that God has for us: that is, a sense of healthy self-esteem, hope, purpose, and direction. The message of Jesus Christ is a message bringing that hope, direction, and personal vitality. As sermons become more relevant, church work also becomes more meaningful, workshops become more helpful, education more life-changing, and people receive hope. People come to see the best in themselves through understanding the best of God's love for them. The amazing grace that comes through Jesus Christ is best experienced as Christ meets us at the point of our personal need and gives us hope.

Of all the means and methods the church has to meet personal needs, the worship service and preaching can be the most powerful. In analyzing the churches in America that are growing, one of the common focuses is that they meet personal needs. Fulton Buntain is pastor of the Life Center Assembly of God Church in Tacoma, Washington. The church has a program of meeting needs from a full-blown K-12 school to a retirement center. This church, which is one of the largest in the Assembly of God fellowship, focuses clearly upon meeting personal needs. The preaching of Ed Young at

Fellowship Church in Dallas, and his father, Edwin Young, at Second Baptist Church in Houston is needs-based preaching. Whether it's the creative, flamboyant style of the son, or the more traditional style of his father, these two pastors of the largest churches in the Southern Baptist fellowship represent needs-based preaching that grants an unbelievable sense of hope. Tyrone Gordon developed an exciting ministry for a struggling United Methodist Church in Wichita and built it to one of the larger churches in his denomination by responding to the personal needs of people in Wichita, particularly through powerful preaching and relevant worship.

Of all the perspectives on needs-based evangelism, that which is most powerful is when the needs are personal. The most powerful needs to which the church can minister are those at the core of the individual.

CHAPTER 10

HOW TO WITNESS, OR PERSONAL EVANGELISM

What, Me Witness?

For many laypeople, being told by a pastor or a church leader that we all need to witness for our faith is one of the most predictable turnoffs possible. So many Christians are just repulsed by the idea of witnessing or any form of personal evangelism. Although the story of Philip witnessing to the Ethiopian and the Acts 2 description of the followers of Jesus preaching on the streets of Jerusalem and thousands "joining up" are rousing illustrations of the importance of witnessing; for so many Christians, this behavior is something they would absolutely never do. Though there are preachers and laypeople who will stand and give testimonies to the importance of witnessing, for most people, the actual practice of witnessing sounds impossible, even obnoxious.

Many Christians have experienced zealous, evangelistic Christian witnessing. It may have happened at the office, at a party, or even on the street corner. Most of the time, the result for the person being witnessed to is a feeling of anger with the personal commitment never to do that kind of behavior. Too much of the so-called witnessing simply is bragging on oneself: "I'm saved, so what's wrong with you." This attitude is conveyed so often. There is an arrogance about it that is just repulsive. To be "witnessed" to is too often not the beginning of Christian growth and fellowship, but the beginning of anger and resentment. Most mainline Christians do not want to witness under any circumstances.

Teaching Your Congregation to Witness

However, with all of our unpleasant or fearful experiences about witnessing, the Bible is clear that we are called to be his witnesses. The Great Commission tells us that this is our job as followers of Christ. We are told that the limits of our witnessing are the "ends of the earth." Caught in this dilemma, most Christians simply feel guilty. They are caught in the "double bind" of wanting to be loyal and serve Christ, yet absolutely refusing to witness. A kind of spiritual schizophrenia develops. It then becomes imperative that we teach our congregations how to witness in a way that is helpful, possible, and effective.

There are seven basic styles of witnessing that will work in a contemporary high-tech post-Christian story-oriented culture. They are: (1) telling your story; (2) helping; (3) explaining; (4) being and doing; (5) inviting to attend; (6) inviting to accept Christ; and (7) discipling.

Telling Your Story

Even the most reserved personality still has the inner desire to tell his or her own story. We are adept at griping about the situations we face in life. Most people will be glad to tell you about the hard time a clerk gave them at a store or the unfairness of their boss. But there is also within each of us a desire to tell the good things we have experienced. If we bought a great new car, if our Christmas experience was one of the best we ever had, or if we've just returned from vacation and had a great time, we want to tell the story.

Effective witnessing is simply telling your story. It begins with our understanding that the experience of Jesus Christ is the most fantastic thing any human being can have. It begins with understanding that to live as a Christian is not only right, but also joyful, wholesome, satisfying, and successful. Believing that we have a good deal makes it easy to share.

The first aspect of witnessing is simply telling our story. You get to work a little early, fix a cup of coffee, and sit down at your desk with a smile on your face. A fellow employee comes in, "down in the dumps," and responds to you. You give back a smile and a little encouragement. The other employee asks you, "Why are you so happy?" Now, the door is open. Without being arrogant or obnoxious, just say something like, "Yesterday, I was in church. It was a fantastic sermon, a great worship experience. When I worship God it just makes me feel better. I have always found that being a Christian just works in a positive way." The response does not take a complicated theological explanation. It is just a testimony of the simplest kind. The response from the friend usually is simple. It may be a question, a comment, or a long conversation. Story-telling provides an opportunity to tell about Christ in a direct, usable way. Christians need to think about their story, practice their story, and be ready to share.

Helping

One of the most basic ways we witness is by doing what Jesus taught so clearly. It is helping. The good Samaritan model is the model of evangelism that works in today's society. It is built on a concept of not only helping, but also building a relationship. It starts with paying attention; that is, listening and noticing your friends, family, business associates, and customers. Sense where they are hurting, what struggles they are going through, and be ready to listen and help.

It's relational evangelism in the best way. It is nonjudgmental, accepting, and Christlike. It's giving in the most satisfying kind of way. When we help, we need to be ready to use other forms of witnessing, such as telling our story, explaining the faith, and inviting. Witnessing by showing the model of Christ's love is one of the most authentic ways to convey the gospel.

Helping can be offered as simple acts of kindness. Often, churches across America have seen that doing an act of kindness such as handing out bottles of water at a public event, cleaning up trash that has been neglected, or visiting the elderly at a nursing home becomes a means of showing the world that Christ calls us to help. The name of a church on a bottle of water given free at a public event can be the opportunity to witness when no other opportunities seem to be present.

The concepts of needs-based evangelism in this book are all about helping. When we help, Christ is seen. When we help and add the other means of witnessing, such as explaining, inviting, and telling our story, people are led to Christ, and the church grows.

Explaining

A third way, a partner with the first two, is explaining. We live in a world where everyone seems to be secular and yet everyone speaks about being so spiritual. Because of this pseudo-spiritualism, there are lots of conversations about religion, spiritual matters, God, faith, and religious practices. In those conversations, a well-informed, compassionate, nonarrogant, loving Christian can make a great witness by just being prepared to explain. To be an explainer, you need to be a good theologian, a loving listener, and have a nonargumentative style.

In our post-Christian age, questions arise such as, "Why don't Christians baptize the same way?" "I've always wondered why there are so many different dominations?" "Can't Christians get along together?" "What's the difference between a Muslim and a Christian?" "What do Christians believe about alcohol, politics, or abortion?" Good compassionate answers can lead to healthy conversations about the faith and an opportunity to invite or tell your story or even help.

Being and Doing

Even the most bashful of us all can show our faith in what we do. Even those of us who feel inarticulate and fumble with words of explanation can be witnesses in our actions. By the way we show love, by the way we help others, by our honesty and integrity, by living out the model of Jesus, other people will see Jesus in us. All Christians witness by example whether we mean to or not. Of all the ways to witness, witnessing by example is the most basic; whether we are telling a story, explaining the faith, or helping someone in need, our example needs to be one of integrity. Without that integrity, any form of witnessing is not effective. This means that we take Jesus' words seriously and love one another as Christ loves us by building people up with our words and deeds, by being patient and kind, and by being the first to admit wrongdoing.

Inviting to Attend

One of the simplest ways to witness is to invite. Churches offer lots of opportunities to invite. Invite your friend to worship. Invite someone to Christmas Eve services. Invite your relatives to join you on Easter. These are normal times that people want to go to church: Christmas and Easter. More and more, we are finding today that people want to go to church on Christmas Eve. Most people will say yes to a friend's invitation.

To invite someone, we need invitational opportunities. For churches to grow, the church needs to provide many opportunities for the invitation to be made. Churches should plan events that are more than just another thing to attend, but that are an authentic part of the church's mission and purpose.

A concert can be an open door for someone. One of the strongest Christians I know, a physician, was led to Christ out of his secular world when his son was invited to a concert by some friends. His son went to the concert and invited his sister, and she went to the concert. They got involved in the youth program. They eventually invited their dad to another concert. The dad came more and more with his kids. The children accepted Christ and were baptized, and eventually the father did too! It became a journey of faith for him, and now he leads strongly in the church and is an evangelistic layperson. It might never have happened if there hadn't been a concert that his teenagers wanted to attend.

Many invitational opportunities are also opportunities for ministry. A woman who has lost her husband in death is invited to a grief workshop. A mom who is having trouble parenting her teenagers is invited to parenting training at the church. A young single is invited to a volleyball game at the church. All of those invitations can lead to more opportunities for witnessing, more growth, and, literally, a place for Christ to affect their lives.

Inviting to Commit

The last form of witnessing is another kind of invitation. This invitation is not to attend, but an invitation to accept. Finally, in the course of witnessing, we need to learn how to make the most important invitation, and that is to invite your friend to accept Jesus Christ as his or her Lord and Savior.

Anyone in sales knows that you have to "close the deal." It seems hard sometimes, and yet, if the other witnessing has been done, the final invitation is easy. It just represents unlatching the door so that a person can step into the presence of Christ. It can be a simple, short sentence such as, "I sense that you are really ready to accept Jesus Christ as your Lord and Savior."

It may be a more complicated invitation: "We've talked many times about the church and faith. I would like to talk to you tonight about what it means really to accept Jesus as your Lord and Savior." The invitation may be in the midst of crisis. "I know you are having a hard time, but I sense in the things you have been saying to me that you want to be closer to God than you have ever been before. Maybe now is the time to make that commitment, to get things straightened out between you and God."

However the words are said, someone needs to make the invitation. Oftentimes the opportunity comes without us planning or ever thinking about it. We simply need to be ready.

Discipling

We have long understood that becoming a mature Christian is a process. There certainly are decisions that are important to that process; and yet, for most of us, it is a process of development and learning and growing. It is a process that involves being a part of the Christian community. Therefore, one of the most effective ways to witness is to help a person grow in the faith. We witness by supporting a person's involvement in a regular Bible study group, support group, accountability group, prayer group, or Sunday school class. Most people today make a decision for Christ after being a part of a Christian community over a period of time long enough to learn, understand, and experience the validity of Christian community. Being the teacher, the friend, and the class leader are ways in which each person witnesses and leads others to come to know Christ.

The methodology of telling, helping, explaining, being, doing, inviting, and discipling are viable, authentic, practical ways that the church can witness today. These simple concepts help us all understand that witnessing is not a strange thing to do, but a natural thing to do. Any church that seeks to lead new people to Christ must teach its members how to be witnesses.

Christians in churches that are truly evangelistic must naturally tell their story, help others out, explain the theology, and invite others to events and activities and, most important, to Jesus Christ.

Personal Christian witnessing is natural, effective, and enjoyable.

CHAPTER 11

EVENTS IN NEEDS-BASED EVANGELISM

Events Work

In our society, one of the hardest problems in reaching secular people is finding the door—that is, the opportunity or the way to present the truth. Even when people are deeply involved in transition and looking for answers, they will not necessarily show up at the church. Most mainline church members are reluctant to witness, share their faith, or do any form of personal evangelism, except they will invite if there's a reason. It is hard for long-term mainline Protestant members to just invite someone to church. And for most secular people in our society, going to a church that they may perceive as boring, irrelevant, and misguided is not an easy sell. So we need a point of hospitality, a way to open the door, a way to pry open receptivity, a way to touch the need.

Needs-Based Events

If a church is committed to needs-based evangelism, it is ready to meet the need. The invitation can oftentimes come as an invitation to an anger management workshop, a parenting of teenagers class, a divorce adjustment program, a grief management program, or countless other ministries designed to meet needs. In the case of events, the invitation is directly to a program to meet a particular need. When the crisis or transition is heavy—a deep depression from the death of a spouse, debilitating anger over a divorce, bewildering frustration over a teenager out of control—people will respond more directly to the church's offer for help. Meeting the need is an opportunity to bring the new person into the fellowship. Because the friends of most devout, committed church members all go to church already, opportunities are needed that will reach beyond the core of the active church members' friends to peripheral persons.

Events evangelism is a powerful way to provide that opportunity for contact, hospitality, and involvement. It provides an opportunity to start the process of meeting the needs and leading someone to the healing power of Jesus Christ. Events should be well planned, needs-directed, interesting, exciting, manageable, quality, and authentic to the gospel of Jesus Christ.

Churches, over the years, have used many events to reach more people. In rural America, the old-time revival meeting was held, and lots of people came. A potluck supper was organized on a Sunday evening, and even the most cantankerous wanted to taste a good old-fashioned church potluck supper. A summer picnic at the park captured many a reluctant sinner. Today, the events need to be different—concerts of all types of music are beautiful to reach new people. Those concerts, if planned well and managed well, will pay for themselves. Interesting guest speakers discussing contemporary topics are opportunities for invitations. General fellowship and community events can be opportunities to reach new people—craft shows, arts festivals, Halloween parties, car shows, health clinics, block parties, or almost any kind of event that is entertaining and helpful can bring new people to the church.

The important issue in all the variety of events that may be used to reach new people is that they must always be consonant with the mission and purpose of the church. These events must include hospitality, love, care, help, and good information; and authentic sharing of the faith must always be a part of the event. For the event to include sharing of the faith, it must include authentic hospitality so that persons who come to the event sense the spirit of Christ's love in the churchpeople they meet.

Quality Events

The church must make every effort to work out every detail of hospitality from the greeting at the door to a follow-up letter to careful signs for the designated location and process of the event. Everything must be done well. Secular people today expect quality and will be turned off by bungling of the church. The church is on trial today; and we must understand that, to bring the gospel, we must be willing to remove all the blocks of prejudice and skepticism present in our society. We must also understand that we are in a world that is highly competitive for time and energy. Events must be done well. We compete today with all the secular choices. The church that is committed to reaching new people can do events evangelism well. There can be a great deal of joy and a tremendous amount of opportunity for involvement of the laity in events.

Events become, for the congregation, a way to mobilize the energy of the church in a fun and often exciting, rewarding way for the participants. Events, in themselves, are enjoyable not only for the visitor, but also for the longtime member. Events are authentic in terms of celebrating the values of the committed congregation. There is a satisfaction in having a healthy, positive Halloween party that affirms the church members' ministry of caring for the needs of the community. It affirms validity of the life of the church in the community. The organization of an exciting contemporary concert provides not only a way for an individual to invite some non-church friends to church, but also a great worship experience for the individual.

Events provide an opportunity for the congregation to become significant within the community. One advertising concept has to do with the perceived position of an organization or an idea within the community. So often, the mainline church is at the bottom of the list—the last place to go. As we hold increasingly helpful, entertaining, exciting events, our position within the community rises. In the old days, following the

Second World War, the church found itself in one of the top positions in the community. It was easy to invite. People wanted to be at this popular place—the church. Today, people don't want to be at the church, particularly the mainline Protestant church. Our task is changing this and leading people to experience a repositioning of the church in the minds of the secular world. Instead of being the brunt of a joke in a television sitcom, we need to be the positive conversation in the informal times in our corporate break rooms.

Creative Events

In developing the events, congregations need to be careful to see not only that they are well planned, but also that we consider all the creative possibilities. Some events can be combined with others. Some events become a natural flow of the church's position in the community. Events become the natural response for problems and difficulties within the community. Creativity, innovation, and lots of congregational planning and dreaming are essential. Publicity and advertising are crucial for events evangelism as well as ministry evangelism and worship evangelism.

A congregation decides to hold a Halloween party to give an opportunity for kids to be off the street and in a controlled, safe environment. In the creative thinking about the Halloween party, the group decides that it might be well to get involved in a pumpkin sale to raise money for missions and, at the same time, use the pumpkin sale to point toward the Halloween Fall Festival. The youth selling pumpkins and adults preparing for the Halloween party become a means of developing excitement within the congregation. Local preschools and other children's groups that come to the pumpkin patch for pumpkins and storytelling hear about the Halloween party. In all of this, people experience a valid October event and the church's witness is enhanced.

Always in events evangelism, getting the names of participants is crucial. Sign-in registrations and attendance books can be helpful. One of the key ways of getting names is to offer a door prize. A simple offering of a door prize gives names and information that's crucial.

Test for a Good Event

For successful needs-based evangelism events, there are some basic things that need to be reviewed. First, does the event meet needs? Is it authentic and consonant with the gospel of Jesus Christ—that is, as Christ called us to be like the good Samaritan and respond to needs, does the event do that? Is it authentic in that way, and not manipulative or superficial?

A Saturday morning event for single parents and their kids involved games for the kids, free medical treatment for families, a car clinic for car repair, and an opportunity for the singles' group to witness and invite the single parents to activities. It targeted the major needs of single parents. It was fun. It was an opportunity to witness.

The second test is whether the gospel is presented clearly in the invitation made to participate in the life of the church. Events need to be sponsored by single local churches, not by groups. In order for the gospel to be presented clearly, it needs to be done in the context of the local church Christian community, where persons can get acquainted, come back the next week, sense the support system of the local church, and understand the event is surrounded by worship, Christian education, caring and loving fellowship, discipleship training, and the other full programs of the local church. When the event is done in a local church setting, the gospel can be proclaimed much more clearly. Most events can be done without a high cost. Most events can be achieved through lots of volunteers and lots of involvement. Many local organizations will contribute to special events. Some events, such as concerts, guest speakers, and so on, will involve a ticket or a fee in order to attend.

Workshops and Programs

Workshops and programs can also be understood as long-term events as opposed to one-time events such as a concert. One of the strongest programs I have observed is the divorce adjustment workshop. There is no situation in American life that is more difficult, more painful, and needs more help than divorce. For the mainline Protestant church to be available without judgment, but to offer God's beautiful grace in the midst of this traumatic time, is one of the most productive opportunities for reaching new people for Jesus Christ. Divorce workshops that center upon a non-judgmental attitude and a sense of welcoming hospitality can be powerful. Divorce adjustment workshops should not be done ecumenically, but should be done by a local church, so that, as people participate in the workshop, they'll automatically become acquainted with local singles and local members of the singles' Sunday school class within the church, and also be integrated into the loving fellowship of the church.

Workshops for widows and widowers have the same kind of opportunity as divorce adjustment workshops. They meet a need at a critical time. Workshops such as the divorce adjustment workshop or the widow and widower workshop should be followed up with the creation of a support group, an opportunity to meet regularly at the church, to follow up on the ideas of the workshop, to develop community with the other members of the church and the Christian community, and to be led in the discipling process of Christian growth.

The need for help in a multitude of ways offers so many workshop opportunities—workshops for grandparents rearing grandchildren or workshops for people dealing with cancer. Workshops on parenting preschoolers are desperately needed today. Workshops to enrich marriages and help couples make decisions and deal with conflict are desperately needed. One of the most acute needs in our society today is the need for anger management. All of these workshop events can provide not only an event centered around several days or weeks, but also a follow-up support group and involvement in the Christian community. They are some of the most effective ways of needs-based evangelism.

CHAPTER 12

QUALITY INDIGENOUS WORSHIP MEETS NEEDS

The Worship Wars

Mary is in her eighties. She had gone to church all her life and been a member of her present church since the church was organized forty-two years ago. When the new pastor said, "We have to start a contemporary worship service," she said loudly, "No!" Mary was angry and upset about changing the worship in her church. Several of the members of the congregation said that the church needed music that would reach the younger generation. In the heat of the board meeting, Mary said, "If they want that kind of music, they can go to a bar. They are not going to play drums and guitars in my church."

Bill is thirty-eight. He and his wife, LeAnn, have three children. They want to get back to church. He was in a major accident at work, and the time in the hospital was traumatic. He made some promises to God about getting his family back to church. So, they are shopping. Bill and LeAnn are shopping for a church. Both of their parents are attending classic mainline Methodist and Presbyterian churches. They visited their parent's churches; the kids said it was boring. Bill and LeAnn agreed! So they were visiting different churches, to keep the promise to get the family back to God. They visited a "community church" across town. His dad called it a Willow Creek clone. It didn't matter. He loved the music. They did a drama. The kids thought it was fantastic. They had all kinds of activities for children and youth. But what attracted the whole family was the worship service. They showed video clips, and there was an outline of the sermon, and even the kids could answer the questions that were on the outline. There was a separate bulletin for the children, and kids participated in the leadership of the service. The whole family decided that's where they were going to church.

Churches, individuals and new Christians are caught in the worship wars. How to worship God? What is the right kind of music, the best kind of music? What should the liturgy be like? Do you sing the old hymns and say the old creeds? Is there an overhead presentation that goes with the sermon? Is there a drama? Will the children and youth lead and participate in worship? These are some of the questions. If the church is to reach people of the twenty-first century, the worship *must meet needs*.

Indigenous Worship

The question is not whether worship is traditional, contemporary, blended, or post-modern. The question is, Does it work? Does it meet needs? Are persons brought to Jesus Christ? Is the message of the gospel proclaimed authentically and in a way that it changes people's lives? The measure of quality worship is not in the academic-sounding words of the sermon or the polished voices of the music leaders; the measure is what happens to the individual who worships. It is indigenous worship.

They called it blue jeans worship. It wasn't contemporary; it wasn't traditional. It was blue jeans worship. When I heard about blue jeans worship at FUMC at Fort Gibson, Oklahoma, I thought the Reverend Ray Crawford had gone too far. Not at all. Ray had gone just the right distance. He was doing worship that worked in that eastern Oklahoma small town. Blue jeans worship is just what many people in that town needed. It was where they were. The worship used music and symbols and feelings that related to the needs of the people in that town. The goal of worship today is to relate to the needs of the persons worshiping. It is indigenous worship.

The goal of worship, preaching, liturgy, and music is to bring together the power of the gospel of Jesus Christ to the needs of people in the pews or the chairs or the benches. Our task is worship that is authentic in the truth of the gospel and authentic for the needs of the people. When worship is authentic in both ways, evangelism happens. Worship that deals with the hurts and hopes of the people in the community where the work is happening is worship that will reach new people. The test questions are: Did the liturgy lead the participants to the throne of God? Did the music proclaim the truth of the message of Jesus? Did the sermon presentation sense the real hurts, hopes, and dreams of the congregation? The goal of needs-based worship that is truly indigenous is in no way a sell-out of the authenticity of the gospel, a compromise of any biblical truth or a perversion of any doctrine. The task of indigenous worship is that the great Christian, biblical message is made understandable, experiential, and helpful to the participant in worship.

Walt Kallestad, pastor of Community Church of Joy, along with the laity of his Lutheran church, demonstrated the power of indigenous worship as they created worship that truly met needs. This church in Phoenix is one classic example of a mainline Protestant church becoming entrepreneurial in its style, missional in its purpose, evangelistic in its results, and indigenous in its worship style. Kallestad's staff led the congregation in developing what many call contemporary worship, but it is simply worship that meets the needs of the people in Phoenix. In the process, they also created one of the largest churches in the Lutheran denomination.

Not far across the Phoenix Metropolitan area, Tommy Barnett, pastor of First Assembly of God Church, has modeled the same combination in a different denominational setting. The ministry of the First Assembly of God Church is one focusing upon needs. They have one of the strongest ministries to the homeless community in Phoenix. At the same time, their ministry to children, youth, and adults is second to none. The model of caring for the poor, established by Tommy Barnett in Phoenix, became the model for one of the most exciting and effective ministries to the poor in Los Angeles, pastored by his son, Matthew. The worship of the Assembly of God

Church in Phoenix and its spin-off church in Los Angeles meets the needs of hurting people. It is dramatic, entertaining, strongly experiential; and it relates to the people.

Janet Forbes was pastor of First United Methodist Church in Cheyenne, Wyoming. This congregation, with a great tradition of leadership within the Cheyenne community and honoring traditional music, found joy as Janet introduced an intergenerational worship during which the children were involved in the worship service and the families felt an affirmation. More and more, the congregation became younger, and her persuasive leadership added creativity and joy to worship that reached people who had never come to that classic church before. The primary time of entry to the church today is when needs are met. Most often, wherever that door to the church is, it must include the door to worship. Without needs-based worship, many of our other needs-based evangelism programs are blunted in their effectiveness.

Preaching

Effective preaching is one of the clear characteristics of indigenous worship. The task of bringing the Word of God to the people is a task not only of clear exegesis and exposition of the Word, but also of a clear understanding of the people who are hearing the Word. The characteristics of the great and effective preachers of the Word in the growing Protestant church are all the same. Whether it is Robert Schuller, Joel Osteen, Bill Hybels, Kirbyjon Caldwell, Adam Hamilton, Rick Warren, Craig Groeschel, or Joyce Meyer, the preaching style is the same. It is based upon the needs of the listener. It is experiential, indigenous. It fits with the people. It centers around experiences that the listener understands and can relate to. The preaching is needs-based. Analyze the sermon topics, the style, the illustrations, the sequence of ideas, and certain things become clear.

Needs-based preaching must be well done. It should relate well to the learning patterns of the congregation, the experience of the congregation, and the needs of the congregation. It is delivered in a way that is appropriate to the congregation. It may be enhanced with a video clip of an interview of a man on the street done in Chicago and shown as part of the worship at Willow Creek, or an engaging story out of the experiences of Schuller or Kirbyjon. It may be enhanced with the high-tech worship of Mike Slaughter at Ginghamsburg United Methodist Church or with the fantastic music at Christ Church in Nashville or the simple, practical stories of Joel Osteen at Lakewood Church. Bob Russell, pastor of the Southeast Christian Church in Louisville, Walter Kimbrough, pastor of Cascade United Methodist Church in Atlanta, and Jim Capps, pastor of the Southport Presbyterian Church in Indianapolis, all model practical needs-based preaching. The preaching that is reaching Americans today is preaching that is practical, usable and relates exactly to where the people are. It is biblically sound and doctrinally authentic, and people all across America are rushing to hear these great preachers. The lesson that all of us who stand in the pulpit must learn from those who are leading in effective preaching today is to make it relevant, well-delivered, entertaining, biblically sound, doctrinally authentic, intellectually developed, and visually punctuated.

Craig Groeschel left. He once served as Associate Pastor of First United Methodist Church in Oklahoma City. He now pastors one of the fastest growing nondenominational churches in America. Based upon our old theories about what makes worship work, one would expect Groeschel's concepts to fail totally. He has started congregation after congregation in various places across the south central United States. The worship is based upon excellent music, local hospitality, and the preaching done by Groeschel, and then is videotaped and played in seven different settings. The total in seven satellites makes it one of the largest churches in America. It would seem illogical that thousands of people would want to worship with the preaching done on a video screen, and yet that is happening. The reason is that Groeschel's preaching is relevant, it meets needs, it is biblically based, and it brings the healing, leading, caring power of Jesus Christ to ordinary people.

Needs-based evangelism is effective only when it is the center of all the church life. Not only an after-school program for latchkey kids or a twelve-step recovery program on Friday nights, it must be the basis of all that is happening in the life of the church, including the preaching and the worship.

Multiple Worship Services

One of the most creative ways churches today are meeting needs through worship is through multiple worship services. Because of the diversity of needs and diversity of preference, contemporary churches today, in reaching out to other persons and seeking to bring the gospel and meet their needs, need to be willing to offer a variety of worship services. Sunday morning is not the only time that people can come to worship. Many people work on Sunday and want to attend worship at a different time. Sunday evenings, Wednesday nights, and Saturday nights are common alternatives. Worship services need to be available at more than one time; 8:00 Sunday morning, 11:00 Sunday morning, or 2:00 Sunday afternoon are powerful opportunities. Sites need to be varied. Some services can be in the sanctuary, some in an informal setting in the gym. Music should be different. The sermon can be videotaped and fed or taken to different sites. Preaching can be done by a variety of ministers on staff or by the same minister on staff. Our goal is to meet the needs of people, and that's done with a variety of services.

The Kwang Lim United Methodist Church in South Korea is the largest Methodist church in the world. On one occasion several years ago, I spent a week with my wife and son at Kwang Lim just learning and watching. The pastor, Sundo Kim, taught me so much. He was patient and precise. He preached on Sunday four times with lunch in between the third and fourth service. They had four services on Sunday not only for space but for convenience. After that experience, it was clear to me that multiple services are a significant part of the answer.

Kent Millard pastors St. Luke's United Methodist Church in Indianapolis. They have thirteen services each week. Four of these are at two off-site campuses, nine at the main campus, including traditional, contemporary, blended, Taizé prayer service, and a prayer for healing service (once a month). They have pioneered multiple services with multiple focuses, all seeking to meet needs and to bring people to Jesus Christ.

Different services and different styles of worship are all part of reaching new people for Christ.

Music

One reality of human life is choice. God has given us the gift of choice. One of those choices is the music we like. Indigenous worship allows us to choose that. Too often, the church has said what music is spiritual. It's as if we're trying to say, "Jesus likes only contemporary music" or "Jesus likes only old-time gospel music" or "Jesus likes only classical fifteenth-century music." It's silly. All music, if it proclaims the truth of the gospel, and if it relates to the person who listens and experiences worship, is good. When our goal is leading people to Christ, the choice of music is a critical choice. Whether we're dealing with post-modern, G.I. Generation, baby boomer, millenial, or any other generational ministry or cultural ministry, the choice of music helps us in meeting needs. The basic question of music choice has to do with whether or not the needs of the individual are being met and are being led to the throne of God.

With multiple services meeting multiple needs, we must have multiple kinds of music in worship. Classic Christian music is important. Traditional music reaches some. The so-called emerging church worship styles are also important to understand. I'm waiting to hear about a church that has a full-blown cowboy worship service. I grew up in western Oklahoma and would like to hear good gospel music sung with a guitar and a stand-up bass and a little nasal twang to make it authentic. Worship music may vary, but the gospel is the same.

Follow-Up to Worship

All effective indigenous worship that has as its goal to reach new people for Jesus Christ must involve a clear follow-up to participation in worship. Churches devise all kinds of means and methods to get the names of the visitors. In some congregations, to ask a visitor to stand is the worst thing to do; in others, it's the right thing to do. Some congregations have visitor booths at the door, others sign in at the worship service. All kinds of means and techniques are used to help us to get the names of the visitors.

When the names are collected, follow-up contacts must be made; that is, visitors need to be called, sent letters, and sent postcards—whatever technique works to see that a follow-up is made, not only the week immediately after they initially visit, but on subsequent visits. If indigenous worship works well and needs are met, the individual will want to become involved in Sunday school classes, Christian education opportunities, workshops, and church fellowships. Worship must involve the invitation to all of these activities of discipleship, Christian education, and Christian fellowship.

The way in which individuals are led to Christ is through community. Indigenous worship needs to provide every means possible for individuals to become involved in the Christian community so that they will grow in Christ and make their commitment to Jesus Christ as their Lord and Savior.

The Invitation and the Commitment

The most authentic part of worship must be the invitation to become disciples of Jesus Christ. Churches do it differently. Some churches do it best in classes and training programs. Others do it in the spontaneous moment of a revival meeting. However, *every worship service* needs to involve, in some way, the invitation to become a follower of Jesus Christ. Though the worship service may provide significant help in encouragement, peace, satisfaction, joy, repentance, and information, it also must involve a clear invitation to become a follower of Jesus Christ. However it is done, it needs to be effective. There should be no holding back in presenting the plan of salvation and the means to follow that plan!

Worship is often the first place that a new person will visit in a church, whether that person is new in the community or going through a significant transition and looking for a church. Often, they will visit.

Effective, indigenous, creative, and needs-based worship will reach new people. It is very possible that the most effective way in reaching new people with needs-based evangelism is through the worship service and the preaching. In looking at the significant growth in various churches across America in the last ten years, the majority of that growth could be attributed to worship services that meet the needs of people.

CHAPTER 13

MARKETING FOR DUMMIES

Marketing 101

The *Dummies* series of books have caught the attention of America. Whether you're looking for help on selling your home, learning how to use your computer, or investing in the market, there's a *Dummies* book for it. There is even a *Dummies* book on how to study the Bible. Obviously, our desire to learn and to know is being met by those who publish how-to books for people who have little experience. Based upon the marketing of the *Dummies* books, it would seem that there ought to be a book in a series entitled *Marketing Your Church for Dummies*.

He's an experienced church administrator, longtime conference staff. He directs the promotion and publicity materials for a particular mainline Protestant judicatory. And yet, when he wanted to publish a book on how to "sell your church," he found that church publishers refused the title. It does seem obnoxious to talk about marketing the church—after all, it's a spiritual matter. We're called to be evangelists, witnesses. We want to make sure that people know we are godly and holy in our tasks, and so we print our church stationery with very formal typestyles, and we design our buildings to look very "churchy." We develop our own church-related vocabulary to speak of normal things—the stage is a "chancel," the lobby is a "narthex." The task of proclaiming the gospel, however you want to describe it, is basically marketing. That is, if contemporary mainline churches want to reach more persons for Christ, we must learn marketing and learn it well. No longer can we afford to be dummies and to bungle the task, communicate poorly, and turn more people off than we turn on for the gospel.

The advertising and marketing industry has developed into a refined, highly professional science. In the marketing world, we know how to communicate, how to motivate, how to change attitudes, and how to sell. It is time for the mainline church to learn those basics that American industry knows so well. Pastors need to study marketing. Local churches need to encourage their marketing and advertising experts to join the task of helping the church grow. Every congregation, no matter how large or small, has people in it who know how to sell. American enterprises succeed because they sell products and services. The owner of a small restaurant in a rural American town or the manager of a large mall in urban America are both experts in marketing. Every local church has plenty of expertise; our problem is that we don't use it.

Marketing and Needs

The purpose of this book is not marketing, and yet we recognize that there are basic recognizable marketing practices that work. First, marketing is based upon having a product that people believe they need. Needs-based evangelism calls the church to develop its programs and ministries around needs. Any marketing design begins with ascertaining the needs of the customer. If churches can be clear about finding the need and meeting it, they can clearly begin the first step in effective marketing. The story of the good Samaritan is a story of a Samaritan who saw a need and responded. Jesus calls us to be like the Samaritan. Our program in ministry is based upon seeing the needs on the road of life and doing the best we can to meet the need. Whether a children's ministry, a youth ministry, vocational transition, economic difficulties, chronic depression, divorce, self-esteem, goal-setting, or purpose in life—if a church is responding to these basic needs, it begins the first step in effective marketing.

Purpose and Marketing

The initial phase of helping a church understand its mission in meeting needs and communicating this ministry to people who need the gospel of Jesus Christ is for the church to be clear about its mission and purpose. The second part of marketing for a church is crafting a clear evangelistic statement of purpose. A mission statement that is biblically based and clearly articulated is an absolute key. There will be many times when the local congregation wants a retreat from being involved, wants to become self-indulgent and nonresponsive to the hurts of the world, and wants to stop caring about those in need. If the church's mission statement is based upon the teachings of Jesus Christ—the Great Commandment found in Luke 10 and Matthew 22, the story of the good Samaritan, the writings of Paul, Peter, and John—if those biblical statements are clear in a mission statement of a church, then when the moments of wavering come, leaders can call the church back to their purpose. A mission statement needs to be celebrated over and over; the Jeremiah principle suggests it needs to be repeated every twenty-eight days. I have found it needs to be repeated in some way in every sermon, every newsletter, every bulletin. The church symbols, metaphors, and stories must be celebrated, articulated, and rehearsed over and over, or they get lost in the overstimulated deluge of information from the culture that every contemporary person has to sort through.

Advertising

The third aspect in marketing for churches is to let the community know that you have the product or the service to meet *their specific needs*. This is advertising, or communication. Most churches totally neglect the matter of communicating the answer that they possess. Communication then becomes our major task. Communication, in the case of a church's ministries, involves a multiplicity of means and methods.

One of the first ways that the church can communicate the answers it is offering is to make sure that the members know the services and products available at their own church. If church members are sold on the effectiveness of a parenting program, they will invite their friends and neighbors and relatives to the parenting program and, consequently, to the church and to the gospel. Therefore, the first focus of communication is within the church—newsletters, brochures, and flyers are all means to help the church members know. For a congregation to feel good about its ministries of meeting needs, stories need to appear in the church newsletter, in the announcements, and in the sermons. Pastors seeking to help their church understand clearly the priority of meeting needs must continually tell the stories of how the church is doing it.

The Entrepreneurial Church

Fourth, we need to develop decision-making systems that are more entrepreneurial. Bureaucratic churches use more complicated democratic methods to make decisions to the effect that they simply cannot respond quickly to opportunities. Therefore they will also have difficulty using their finances for advertising or anything that seems non-missional. The success of the entrepreneurial churches in America is shown in their attitude and more simple decision-making processes that help them respond more quickly to opportunities and, usually, spend the necessary money to communicate what they're doing.

It was evident that the front sign needed repairs. Doug, the chairman of the Evangelism Committee, went to the Finance Board to ask for the five thousand dollars needed. At the time he asked, finances were tough, and yet, because the Finance Board understood the priority of needs-based evangelism and that the sign was one of the best ways to get the word out with forty thousand cars driving in front of the church every day, they were willing to use some reserve memorial funds for the sign, rather than for other needed repairs. Because the church had made a prior commitment that evangelism was a priority, a democratic organization could operate as an entrepreneurial organization and make a decision quickly, responding to an obvious organizational opportunity. With clear goals, democratic congregations can make quick and efficient decisions. If the priority is reaching people for Christ through meeting needs, decisions, budget allocations, and program priorities can be made much more quickly.

Funding Marketing

A fifth concept of marketing is funding. One of the tough realities of most churches, large and small, is inadequate money for advertising or communications. When the priority is ministry and mission, we, following the purpose of the church, want to spend our money on helping people who are hurting. By understanding the concepts of needs-based evangelism, we understand that when we help the hurting, we open the door for them to find the beautiful grace of God through Jesus Christ and become active members of our churches.

To defend the need for money spent for advertising and publicity is to understand that, without letting the community know of our ministry to meet needs, people's needs are not met, decisions for Christ are not made, and the church dwindles in size and then has less funds, less financial resources, and less people to do the work of ministry. Successful businesspeople know, as is often stated, *you have to spend money to make money*. If you don't communicate your services, people can't receive the help.

Low-Cost Marketing

Sixth, there are ways to advertise without spending lots of money. Every church needs to find effective, low-cost means of communicating the gospel. Local churches can use their built-in resources, many of which are inexpensive, to get the "Word" out. The front sign on any church is one of the most obvious ways because hundreds, if not thousands, of cars pass by. If the sign is attractive, if the words on the sign describe the ministries within the church—that is, how needs are being met—the sign can be a principal means of marketing, for the information is in front of the source of ministry. The sign must be a marquee type and the advertised information changed weekly. Churches that are on main streets have a great opportunity to use the location for an attractive sign to capture people's attention and give the information of events, worship, and ministries that meet needs. Of all the methods and means of marketing, the front sign is one of the first and most effective. It is important to remember that cute sayings and clever slogans are not effective. We need to publicize on the sign the needs-meeting ministries, events, worship, and programs of the church.

Another inexpensive means of publicizing is using members of the congregation to get the word out. Walking neighborhoods, leaving flyers in doors, asking the congregation to mail notes to their friends about events, and leaving flyers and brochures at various public places all work and are inexpensive. Direct mail, if done carefully and with quality, is most effective. Direct mail needs to be planned carefully so that money used for it coincides with needs-ministry events, preaching, workshops, and other special ministries to meet needs. Mailings also need to be planned carefully so that they are sent out at times when people normally will be visiting a church. There are seasons when secular people are more likely to visit the church: before Easter, Easter Sunday, the fall, before Christmas, and Christmas Eve.

Other public media are also inexpensive. Those include cable television and free articles or stories in the public media. Use of cable television is one of the best opportunities to publicize the needs ministry of the church. It's usually inexpensive. A positive way to do this is to purchase used equipment and use volunteers to put the service on cable television weekly. Include in the worship service broadcast commercials about the needs ministries of the church. In most churches, there are lots of volunteers to do this.

The media is always looking for stories. If the local church is sensitive to the needs of the media to have relevant, creative stories, many of these stories will make newspaper, television, or radio. The local church needs to be careful and work closely with the local media representatives, understanding that they need a good story as much as the church needs their good story put out. The best stories that a local church puts out that are committed to needs-based evangelism are stories about the ministries the church is doing. Most media are interested in programs to solve problems in our community. If these programs are done creatively, stories in the newspaper, television, and radio will be produced. Needs-based churches can find lots of free advertising as they get involved in seeking to help the community.

When Christ United Methodist Church in Tulsa was offering support groups for families involved in both Desert Storm wars, television stations were there, and stories were written up in the local newspaper. When a free car clinic for single parents was provided, it made a good story in the local newspaper. When the rate of divorce was announced in the public media as extremely high, reporters were at Christ Church to ask what the church was doing to support marriages.

If the good Samaritan church is sensitive to the needs of the media, a simple phone call to the television stations telling the local media that the church is having a marriage rededication service on Valentine's Day evening, and they'd be welcome to televise it, will certainly provide a thirty-second free advertisement on the local television station about a church caring about marriages. When the television station is looking for pictures of a Christmas Eve service to be made available to the media, it provides a witness in the community and for the church.

The ministries of a good Samaritan church become an advertisement in themselves. When the church helps, word gets out quickly. A divorce adjustment workshop begins to publicize itself. Word spreads quickly about a free class on kindergarten readiness. People tell their friends who are struggling with depression about a series of sermons dealing with self-esteem. The program of a needs-based church becomes publicity in itself.

Marketing and Church People

Seventh, a most effective method of advertisement that is low-cost is to use the people within the congregation as word-of-mouth sources of letting the community know about what is happening at the church. Nancy calls it "break room ministry"; for every ministry event or program that the church has, we create a flyer that can be put in the break room of local companies and corporations. Church members are instructed to take the flyer and post it on the break room bulletin board or in their apartment complex community room, or wherever people would see it. The flyers are also passed out to friends. They're ways to make the invitation. An attractive flyer is an exciting way, for a very low price, we can communicate a lot of information. Of course, the style and good quality of the brochure or flyer makes a significant difference.

In attending a church growth conference several years ago, one of the speakers, Jessica Moffatt, told the story of her church using a simple brochure that described the church and the church's ministries as a witness, as a way to let friends know what's going on. The church believed that, by handing this brochure to a friend or leaving it in a waiting room at a doctor's office, God would use that piece of paper to lead people to the church and to a better life. It worked! Particularly, Jessica used the brochure as a way regularly to teach the congregation about an easy way of witnessing.

Whether it's a break room flyer or a church brochure, it works. Let your congregation do the walking. Direct mail, radio advertising, effective web pages, worship service time on cable television, television ads, and newspaper ads—all are effective ways to get the message out. A church using its marketing expert laity can really make a significant difference in the community for a small price.

Quality Marketing

Eighth, the marketing plan must involve quality. Because of the consumer focus in American society, people judge the validity, effectiveness, and authenticity of so many things by the quality of its initial presentation. Though the church has difficulty in spending big dollars for advertising, it needs to do everything possible to have the highest quality of brochures, newsletters, signs, and facilities. Everything that communicates is important. The church has the resources to overcome financial limitations. In most congregations, there are graphic designers, decorators, or people who have skill in color, form, and fashion. In most congregations, there are volunteers who will paint the walls when they need to be painted, who will lay the tile, or who will clean the yard. If a congregation is motivated to reach new people for Christ, there are the members who have skills and talents to provide quality advertisement and hospitality as well as quality ministry. For the church to do effective marketing, anyone within the congregation who is skillful in any aspect of marketing needs to be given the opportunity to help and serve. This means that, even though people might not see themselves as professional graphic designers, if they have a talent for layout design and balance, ask them to help. Even if the individuals never went to college and studied marketing, but they own a small business that is very successful in your community or any successful establishment, they know how to market. Ask them to help.

Appearance

Ninth, a major aspect of the quality of marketing has to do with the appearance of the church. Churches are notorious for neglecting their appearance. For good theological reasons, we have said the ministry and the helping come first. The broken windows, walls that need to be painted, and dirty carpets are not as important as the message of Jesus. Certainly that is true, but today's shoppers see the broken, the unpainted, and the dirty first and perceive the church is not authentic. Therefore, the seemingly superficial becomes the means by which the individual finds the important values of the faith. We must paint, clean, remodel, redecorate, and create an attractive, comfortable, welcoming facility.

Two places in a church that need the most attention in terms of quality are the restrooms and the nursery. If a young mom takes her child to a nursery where the facilities are clean and up-to-date, where the nursery worker has a smile and looks her in the eye, where precautions for security and safety are done in a spirit of hospitality, the young mom is impressed and will probably be back.

They had been active members of our church for years. After their first child was born, he was brought to church with his parents every Sunday. Yet on one Sunday, when they came back to get him, he was in a crib, alone in a nursery room. For one moment, the nursery worker had stepped out. They then made a decision not to come back based upon that mistake in the nursery. That's not an isolated story, but it's a reminder of where the priorities are for young American families.

Hospitality

The tenth aspect of marketing has to do with hospitality—that is, people want to be welcomed, and they want to sense the love of Jesus Christ when they walk in the door. They need to sense that they are accepted, loved, and will have a part in the church. There need to be systems of greeting, ushers with smiles, doors that open easily, and signs that tell people where to go. Visitors need to sense a welcoming that is not obnoxious or overdone. Most visitors don't want to stand and be recognized in worship; they want to come in, test the place, and see if they want to stay. At the same time, most visitors appreciate a smile, a spirit of welcoming and hospitality by the worship leader or the greeter at the door. Great effort needs to be taken to convey that spirit of hospitality. A new widow may be helped greatly by a grief workshop, yet she will never return to grow in her faith because of a rude leader, dirty restrooms, or obnoxious Sunday school leader.

Positioning

Eleventh, in understanding marketing, we need to understand several simple concepts, such as positioning and attitude change. To understand how the church's ministry of meeting needs can be known and experienced in the community, it is important to understand a concept that might be called positioning. That is, communities and individuals tend to put things in rank order. That is, they decide that Japanese cars are best and German cars are second best, and American cars are third, and Korean cars are fourth. We tend to give authority and recognition and to relate to that positioning that we put into our minds about institutions and organizations, products, services, and churches. In Small Town, USA, a new independent Bible church at the edge of town was once known as a place where most people would not go. The old Presbyterian church downtown was positioned as the place where people were going. Today, the positioning is completely reversed. The new Bible church meeting in a large, metal building is the place to go, and few attend older downtown churches.

The effectiveness of changing the church's position in the community has to do with the effectiveness of reaching new people and offering the services of care. There are all kinds of ways to help the church move up the positioning ladder. Most of the ways in which things are changed in the positioning has to do with personal values, what socio-economic group people are in, and how those people receive information. The twenty-eight-year-old may experience a church in a very positive way because of its Web site, while the forty-three-year-old single mom may experience the church as positive because of the single parent support group at the church. The way in which the local media experiences the church, and the way the stories in the local newspaper may be written about the church help the church's position. Pastors and lay leaders who want their church to reach new people need to work actively to have good relationships with the media. Most small communities still write news stories about things that are happening at churches, if the stories are newsworthy, interesting, and tell something new.

I remember the church page editor of the local Tulsa paper telling me "never send me another story about your choir." She said every church in town has a choir. Send her something that's newsworthy. I listened to what she said, and it worked. Before we submitted articles to the newspaper, we always looked at the article from the newspaper editor's point of view. Was this a story that the newspaper needed—not just, was it a story that the church needed. By responding to the needs of the newspaper, the newspaper became positive in their feeling about the church, and they put more stories in about the church. If we had a human interest story or unusual thing that happened at the church, a different kind of ministry that had not been done before, we actively provided information for the newspaper. We realized they had news that they needed, and we would enjoy greater publicity.

How to Sell

Twelfth, church leaders, as business leaders, must learn how to sell. We must understand something of how to influence people to respond positively to our message. It is not offensive to understand that an aspect of evangelism is persuasion, presentation, encouragement, and influencing. We are leading people to Christ. This is sales.

We need to learn these basic approaches to sales, motivation, or influencing others. People buy things because other people are buying them. People like things because they are associated with something else they already like. People feel positively about something that meets their needs. We relate well to communications or advertising that makes sense or is logical. We feel positively about something that provides a reward, and we feel negatively about things that do not provide a reward. We are highly motivated when we feel emotionally positive about something. We are motivated to act out of guilt and fear.

We feel good about a product, idea, or experience that relates to our positive feelings about relationships, family, or home. A local church offers stronger marriages for those who take a marriage class.

When half of her bridge club told her that they were going to the Christmas Eve services at Christ Church, she and her husband decided to go too. They followed the group. When the kids at school were talking about a local disc jockey at a Methodist youth group, lots of kids decided to attend with the others. We need to understand the influence of the group and momentum.

If a postcard or brochure from a church has a brightly colored picture of people enjoying themselves on the cover, people tend to read that postcard or brochure because of positive feelings toward the picture. When we have preconceived positive feelings about one thing that is associated with something we are neutral about, usually the positive gets transferred to the neutral.

A billboard on a busy street presented the cause of Christ and the activities of a particular church in a very logical, sensible way. Lots of people responded positively to that simple logic. A radio advertisement promised that if you would attend a particular church, you would get information that could help you deal with major issues of parenting adolescents. People came because they wanted that reward.

When Chuck said, "We don't need any new people in our church. We are comfortable like it is," his friend, Alan, asked him, "Do you believe in Jesus Christ?" Chuck said, "Yes, of course," in an angry voice. Alan said again, "Do you believe in doing what Jesus taught?" Chuck was short as he responded back and said, "Of course, I do." Alan said, "Really?" Chuck said, "Yes." So the friend opened up the Bible to Matthew 28 and read Jesus' instruction: go, teach, and share. Chuck thought about it for a while, and he said, "I was wrong. I want to do what Jesus taught even if I am uncomfortable with all these new people." One strong feeling for Jesus can change a lot of negatives about evangelism.

We change because of a positive experience—that is, it feels good, it's pleasant, it works. We buy cars that run well. We use dish soap that cleans well. We want a positive experience. When we meet needs in a quality way for people—to find help for their depression, encouragement for their purpose in life, satisfaction for their decision for Christ—they want to make a commitment and become a part of the fellowship of the followers of Jesus.

Just as we buy things because of reward or satisfaction, we also are motivated by punishment and fear. Some churches use guilt, fear, and punishment as a major motivation. It is effective under some circumstances. The reality of our life calls us to want to find meaning and hope. The cancer patient who has been told he has but a few years to live is motivated to find salvation. The American citizen afraid of possible terrorist attacks rethinks what is important and what is not important. The retired person, considering her own finiteness, is much more motivated to think about the message of Jesus Christ. The negative does motivate and can be a part of the realistic way in which we meet needs and help people find the wonderful joy of being a follower of Jesus Christ.

Summary

So often, church leaders are reluctant to see evangelism as marketing; and yet, in a practical way, that is what it is. Our job is to let people know about Jesus Christ and his church and to persuade them to commit to follow Christ.

Our job, as was Jesus' job, is to meet the needs of the people in our community and to lead them to God. If we want to do that more effectively, we must market our product of grace from God enthusiastically and persuasively. This could be called sales.

THE HEALTHY CHURCH AND GROWTH

Out the Back Door

I was asked to speak at a county seat church in eastern Oklahoma. The pastor had, a few years before, been a member of our congregation. Ron had since met the educational and theological requirements for being a United Methodist pastor and was now serving his first church. He was enthusiastic and hopeful. He had invited me to come and preach for him for three evenings in a row.

The first evening, the church was full and it was delightful. The second evening, attendance seemed somewhat sparse. After worship, we talked about the church. As we talked about the church, he celebrated the leadership of this congregation with an average attendance of 150. Things were going good. He was feeling great about his ministry except for one thing. People were leaving. They were leaving to join a new independent church that had just built a big new metal building at the edge of town. He was frustrated because even some of his most loyal members had started visiting from time to time. The independent church was booming and growing rapidly. People who had never gone to church in years were going to the new church. Lots of people who were members or had previously been active in the other churches across the town were going to the new church. Baptist, Presbyterian, Assembly of God, Lutheran, and United Methodist were all attending this new independent Bible church. They had creative, exciting worship. The pastor had a style that seemed really to attract people. The church was doing things to make a difference, to help.

After the second night of preaching, leaders of the church asked if they could talk to me. The basic question was, *How do we stop people going out the back door?* They indicated that the church in this stable community did not experience a whole lot of growth, but they were growing some, and they felt good about it. Yet as they grew, people were leaving. Even some of the longtime active members were leaving. *What do we do to stop it?*

The answer to this question is not just an answer for churches in rural America. It's a question that any church is dealing with! We live in a society where there is no loyalty. It is consumer-driven, and we have taught ourselves that we need to go where the best deal is and for the cheapest price. People are not loyal to the brands and products they once bought. They are not loyal to their friends and family members. They show disloyalty to institutions and people all across America. Consequently, all churches are having difficulty holding their church members. They go out the back door as fast as we bring them in the front.

Our culture is a throw-away culture, and most people are just simply shoppers. They will attend one church for a while and then another church and then another church. We continually go through major transitions that put us in different situations, jobs, marriages, cities, and relationships. This shopper mentality and rapid change make church loyalty precarious. Yet beyond the reality of many moves and changes in our society, there are some issues that are critical in terms of keeping and developing church members.

Healthy Churches

The first issue has to do with how we receive members. People oftentimes relate to a church without clearly understanding commitment to Christ and the church. It is important that we take time to explain. The church must present itself so authentically that there are no surprises. It's important that we have a time of clear assimilation, in which we, in a variety of ways, develop means to help new members become more closely involved. Churches assign shepherds and sponsors for new members. We have classes on learning your spiritual gifts. We provide sign-up sheets, orientation classes, and a variety of means to help people get involved and not slip away. Good assimilation must be worked at, innovative, and creative. However, good assimilation is not the only answer.

Health of the local church is critical for keeping members. Much has been said and done in recent years about what is the characteristic of a healthy church. Christian Schwarz has done extensive work in what has been called Natural Church Development based upon a whole body of research from Europe to America. Eight characteristics of a church that is effective and strong were developed. They are natural characteristics of a healthy church. When these things are present, the church will grow and be healthy and people will stay with the congregation. Those characteristics are: empowered leadership, gift-oriented ministry, passionate spirituality, functional structures, inspired worship service, holistic small groups, need-oriented evangelism, and loving relationships.

Many groups have developed many other ways of describing an effective congregation. Recently The United Methodist Church General Board of Discipleship developed a system of twelve characteristics that are characteristics of a healthy church. They include: being in touch with God, clarity of mission, worship, small groups for faith information, hospitality and a spirit of inclusion, outreach and mission, stewardship and generosity, forgiveness and conflict, care of facilities, healthy leadership, spiritual leadership, and leadership capacity. Whether we use "healthy churches" or "natural church development," or another system to measure local church vitality, there are some basic keys to understand and develop loyalty, satisfaction, and long-term involvement of church members.

Loyalty and Needs-Based Churches

Needs-based evangelism provides some significant characteristics for a local church to be healthy and to hold their members in a positive way. First, if individuals feel a sense of purpose or direction in the church and experience involvement and purpose of direction, they will tend to express loyalty and consistency. They will be stronger in their giving as well as their serving. When individuals believe in what the church is doing, they are more compliant and resistant to shopping and leaving.

A needs-based church has a sense of mission: making a difference, bringing the kingdom, changing the world, helping the poor, caring for the teenagers, and helping. The list goes on as we count the needs that are being met by active, vibrant local churches. When the church has a sense of mission and purpose and is clearly making a difference, people respond positively and want to stay and be involved.

When churches are built upon strong sharing and caring relationships, people stay. Needs-based evangelism is built upon grace. It is built upon caring. The very roots of loyalty are found in the combination of positive relationships and purpose in mission.

Needs-based evangelism is done with teams of people who work on projects, help the needy, and respond to hurts. People build friendships and relationships that matter and maintain themselves positively over the years. The church that works together stays together.

If the sense of meeting needs is clearly articulated biblically and is biblically affirmed, people sense a real feeling of purpose in the church. It is not a waste of time. It is more than entertainment. It is vital and meaningful. Longtime research by Viktor Frankl and Abraham Maslow has affirmed that to have a sense of purpose and mission in life is to find a deep satisfaction, joy, and health. Therefore, a church with a purpose that is valid and satisfying will cognitively and relationally provide a reason for people to stay.

People stay with organizations when the leadership is strong and clear. Needs-based evangelism is effective when the leadership is clear, mobilized, and visionary. Needs-based evangelism operates with strong laity and strong pastors. With effective leadership, loyalties that last are developed.

Caring for the Congregation

Finally, so many people leave a congregation because their needs are not being met. When classes are ineffective, music is boring, pastoral care is nonexistent, and problems are not solved, people leave. If the congregation has a basic commitment to meeting needs, that commitment not only is targeted on helping niches of community hurt, but also, by its very nature, relates to the ordinary church member. The good Samaritan church is concerned about the hurting people on the road outside of the church as well as the hurting people down the aisle inside the church.

Care Ministry

Churches over the years have developed multiple means to care for their members. Stephen's Ministry and other similar ministries mobilize the laity to make hospital calls and be lay counselors and helpers. Small group ministries provide ways by which people can identify together in common study and accountability. Church school classes become vital ways in which care is offered in small groups, no matter the size of the congregation. Careful systems of record keeping for churches are imperative. These systems of keeping attendance, addresses, and so on keep people from slipping through the cracks. As churches grow, they tend to break into multiple congregations within the larger congregation. Systems need to be in place to care for every one of the groups by staff, by laity, and by one another. One effective means to care for a medium- to larger-sized congregation is to develop a system of making phone calls on every family at least four times a year. A care telephone team is trained and organized to come to the church, have prayer and refreshments, and then call on the members, not asking for money or anything, but offering to pray for concerns. This prayer telephone ministry is a beautiful way to keep in touch with the needs of the congregation, to find out where pastoral care needs are, and to let the congregation know how important they are.

A prayer ministry is another important way in which a church cares for its members—to be willing to pray for one another. Life Center, an Assembly of God Church in Tacoma, Washington, pastored by Fulton Buntain, has hundreds of people on the prayer team praying for the church, praying for the needs, praying for one another. Churches that organize good prayer caring ministries like this generally cultivate a strong loyalty within the church.

A church culture is built upon the concept of the good Samaritan, a problem-solving culture that will solve the problems of a neglected Sunday school class as well as of a neglected street person. It will be ready to respond and mobilize energies of the members to provide food and support for an active church family whose parent was in a car accident, as well as to respond to teenagers in the community with drug problems. Needs-based evangelism is a good Samaritan church, it is a Jesus church, and it works!

CHAPTER 15

THE PASTOR'S LEADERSHIP

Leadership

As we deal with issues within any society, it becomes clearly evident that a key to success over failure, mediocrity over quality, satisfaction over dissatisfaction is leadership. Whether it is corporate America, manufacturing and sales, U.S. and state governments, or a local church, leadership is key. Biblical narratives are filled with stories about how God works with leaders and potential leaders. Any concept or story about evangelism must also be about leadership. For evangelism to be successful, it must involve the leadership of the senior pastor, the staff, the key leaders of the church, and the key leaders of the fellowship and study units within the church such as Sunday school classes, women's and men's groups, youth groups, and so on. All conversation about needs-based evangelism is meaningless unless the leadership of the local church has a clear, strong understanding of how it works and makes a commitment to provide the leadership for it to work.

Whether the church is a large metropolitan church or a small county seat church, whether the church is a marginalized church at the edge of the inner city or a small family-based church in rural America, the key to the success of making disciples of Jesus Christ is the pastor. The pastor must believe, lead, and be an example.

The Pastor as Evangelist

When a congregation is deeply involved in needs-based evangelism, there are many visitors, many people who are a part of the church's life, the church's ministry, and the church's activities. Most of those persons are there because of the ministry of the church to meet needs. Most are open to the gospel of Jesus Christ. Most are in a time of transition where they are vulnerable, thoughtful, and needy. This provides a magnificent, fruitful opportunity for the pastor to be an evangelist.

American pastors generally see their task as organizers, preachers, and teachers. Most of the time, they see their responsibility is to be the visionary, the motivator, the coach, the pastoral caregiver, or the expert, but not the evangelist.

In needs-based evangelism, the pastor must be involved. The authenticity of the gospel of Jesus Christ begins first with the pastor's personal involvement. That personal involvement includes involvement in the ministry of helping and caring and involvement in the witnessing, sharing, and inviting. The pastor does not do everything. However, the pastor is the chief leader of hospitality. This is not to say that the pastor is the only person who asks people to commit their lives to Christ; however, the pastor must clearly lead. The pastor is to be at every needs-based ministry activity. The pastor must authentically be involved. One way that the pastor's involvement must be most clear is being involved in greeting and building community and in talking to people about committing their lives to Jesus Christ.

The pastor is the chief leader and needs to take the responsibility to make the invitation. I have found that the opportunities for making the invitation come in three ways: hospitality leader, personal evangelist, and vision caster.

The Hospitality Leader

The pastor serves as the chief leader of hospitality, shaking hands, greeting people, making friends, showing trust, talking to the children, relating to the youth. In those settings, conversations can be life changing.

It was the annual church picnic. It was so hot. The food line was slow. Everyone was a little restless. She had pastored this church four years. She knew everyone pretty well. She noticed people in the food line who were not members. They were on the visitor list. A couple in line had been involved in a parenting class for teens. Then she noticed two people who had started coming to the AIDS Ministry Team meetings. She realized that the picnic was about evangelism, her personal evangelism, and she needed to speak to every one of those visitors, personally, if she could. In the course of doing that in the heat of the afternoon, she found it provided a fantastic opportunity to talk candidly about faith, church, membership, and baptism. She did not have an opportunity to talk to every one of the visitors, but she talked to most of them, and within the next few weeks, four of them made commitments and became a part of the church.

In the small town where Chad served as pastor, Friday night football and weeknight basketball were fantastic for community excitement and for church evangelism. He worked the crowd, and people knew he was there to be a friend and to make disciples. He supported the hometown team, built relationships, and shared God's love.

He wrote personal notes to many he spoke to at the community gatherings, and they loved it. He knew what was going on and his culture. He used the games as an arena of care and hospitality. He had a list of prospects and suspects for the church, and he continually communicated to let people know of his concern for them.

The Personal Evangelist

Today, it is extremely difficult to visit people in their homes. Only with careful appointments made with persistence can you find the opportunity to call in a home. Because of mistrust, misunderstanding, and vulnerability of sexually misunderstood situations, home visits are dangerous to do. But the telephone is available all the time. I make lots of telephone calls. I call at times I think people will be home. Like the telephone solicitors, I call on Saturday mornings and early evenings. I am friendly and loving, and I clearly identify that I am the pastor of the church they have been visiting. I call them by name. I know as much as I can about the family I am talking to on the telephone. It works. In a short amount of time, I can show God's loving hospitality to a lot of people. Even those who are not available when I call will get the message on the voicemail. That counts! The telephone is one of the most effective means of personal evangelism for the pastor and lay leaders. Of course, there are many other methods that can be adapted to particular situations.

Many pastors find another effective way is to meet in the pastor's study at an appropriate time to discuss the church and commitment in a formalized kind of way. It works for some and can be a way to help deal in depth and in a private way with some of their spiritual needs and significant questions. The important thing is that the pastor is a personal evangelist.

The Vision Caster

For needs-based evangelism to work, there needs to be a unique partnership between the pastor and the lay leadership, a commitment by those key lay leaders to partner together with the pastor. The partnership must be a partnership to grow and a partnership to meet needs creatively. This partnership of pastor and key leaders is a partnership to be the good Samaritan church, a partnership in niche marketing. The pastor's role with the laity must begin with vision casting. As a pastor sees and knows the dream of growth for the church, the pastor lifts it up continually. There is always resistance to growth. People are comfortable with their groups. There is a threat when new people come to be a part of any group. In our church, when our major goal is reaching new people for Christ, making disciples, it seems a contradiction that some would not want new persons to accept Jesus Christ as Lord and Savior and pledge their allegiance to his kingdom. And yet, it is a natural thing for the existing group to resist new people and change. The pastor needs to overcome that by casting the vision, biblically building the concepts so that the laity is reminded continually of their mission, purpose, and task.

The vision casting will need to be done regularly, aggressively, but not arrogantly. It needs to be done in a context of teaching expressed in sermons, letters, newsletter articles, and comments in committee and board meetings. The vision casting can be celebrated by affirming those who are following the vision. The stories in the newsletters should be about successful needs-based evangelism. People and groups who do this well should be affirmed publicly.

Building a Community of Trust

The pastor in partnership with the laity must build conversations and communities of trust and support. This community of trust between the leaders can be cultivated in informal fellowship. Part of that trust is built with fellowship and fun. Part of that trust is built in informal talking about the vision and the methodologies to accomplish the vision.

He was preaching the series on spiritual disciplines. The sermon was about prayer. In the preparation, he realized this sermon needed to have action with it, knowing that some of the most powerful effectiveness of prayer is when it is in a small group, an accountability group. So, in the sermon, Mark suggested that every Sunday school class and other groups in the church should organize prayer and Bible study groups that would be accountability groups. He had written out a guideline for accountability groups about sharing, study, and prayer together. His suggestion, among the others he had presented in this sermon on prayer, was well received. Several of the Sunday school classes immediately organized prayer, Bible study, and accountability groups. It was discussed in the church council, and the council voted to make this a major emphasis for the rest of the fall. Accountability groups were being organized all across the congregation, and there was a great deal of excitement about the effectiveness of these small groups.

It bothered Mark that he, himself, was not in a group. He just never seemed to have the time with his growing congregation. And yet, when the chairman of the church council asked him about his accountability group, Mark was embarrassingly honest and said he had none. The chair said he did not have one either, and they talked together about being too busy or too isolated. They decided to invite other members of the leadership team to join them in creating an accountability prayer group. It worked. At one point, there were twelve in the group. At another point, with there being some changes and some illnesses, there were only nine. Two years later, they were back to fourteen. Not everyone attended every meeting every week, but Mark found that this group served more than one purpose. It was a way in which he could build powerful, prayerful, positive relationships with the key leaders of the church. This group became the source of much discussion about the church's direction. It was a way in which they built together a sense of teamwork that would be expressed later in decisions about evangelism and growth for the congregation.

Successful pastors need to have good relationships with the key laypersons. Relationships that are prayerful and positive can be very powerful for the church.

Permission Giving

A significant partnership between the pastor and the laity involves permission giving. The organization of the church needs to be set in place so that there are structures for affirming people in fulfilling the mission and purpose. As mentioned earlier in this book, the permission-giving organization is extremely important for a needs-based evangelistic program. When the mission is clear, the vision cast, and encouragement present in the life of the church, people will be touched by the spirit of God and will come up with many creative ideas to reach new people.

Most bureaucratic organizations tend to resist new ideas. The task for the pastor in partnership with the laity is to resist resisting new ideas. The answer when a new idea is shared should be some form of affirmation. Informally or formally, the answer should basically be *yes*. Certainly, the *yes* would involve reminding people of the procedure, church mission goals, budget, and the necessary coordination to do any new program. The pastor and key leaders need to seek to encourage individual laypersons and groups of laypersons to do those new ministries that reach out. Trust in the laity and the Spirit of God is sometimes hard when the new idea is really creative or unusual.

Several laypersons in a Sunday school class had an idea for a Hispanic clinic to provide medical help for low-income Hispanic persons in the community. It was something that had never been done in the church. The first and natural answer was *no*. It cost too much. It was too much trouble. We don't have the resources. Why should we do it? The government will do it. The board was about to give a loud *no*. But, when the laity of the Sunday school class shared their dream of ministry to the pastor, he was supportive. He coached the class leaders. The plan actually fit well into the church's mission statement. The idea was to help people who had medical needs. It might eventually offer the possibility of starting a Hispanic Sunday school class or even a Hispanic church in a larger non-Hispanic congregation. As complicated as a medical clinic sounded, the leadership said *yes*. The pastor provided coaching, help, and encouragement to start the Hispanic clinic. Eventually, it became a new satellite church for the larger congregation.

Encourager

The pastor should be the chief encourager, cheerleader, and the one who celebrates the stuff that's done, knowing that attitudes are changed by positive affirmation. Organizations are held together by strong teamwork and positive feelings. The pastor needs to be the chief cheerleader for needs-based evangelism. The pat on the back mentioned from the pulpit, the personal thank-you letters, and personal involvement by the pastor provide that affirmation so desperately needed.

The pastor needs to continue to be the chief evangelist, not speaking about growth and working for growth in order to enhance his or her professional place, but because it is the right thing to do. It is what Jesus commanded and what we must do. The imperative to grow is always in the context of the Great Commandment and the teachings in 1 Corinthians 9. The pastor's leadership should be biblically clear and always encouraging to the laity.

Pastor as Follower

I had felt good, as we, over the years, had set the goals for needs-based evangelism and expressed it in so many different ways. We had started a whole variety of ministries. One of the strongest areas of ministries was Singles Ministry, including a Divorce Ministry and Widow and Widower Ministry. We revamped our Sunday school to be more centered upon the needs of children and their families. We used a rotation curriculum based on children's learning types, focused clearly upon needs. We developed multiple worship services to meet the needs of different generations and groupings.

The leadership of the church was brainstorming concerning a particular fall event that was to be a citywide block party to invite persons from everywhere. It was an invitational event activity. All kinds of things were going to be happening on that fall weekend at the church. In the brainstorming, I felt great about the leadership of the laity in carrying out the vision of being a needs-based evangelistic church. Then someone said, "What about the animals?"

The big weekend was the weekend before Halloween. It included a big Halloween party for kids, a pumpkin festival. This individual said something I was not prepared to listen to. She said, "Why don't we have a blessing of the animals?" She turned to me and said, "Dr. Pierson, have you ever done that?" I paused and gulped. I didn't want to answer. I answered quietly, "No, I've never done it." She said, "Have you ever heard of a church doing it?" Of course, I said yes, it was something done often in some traditions. Then she said, "Don't you think that this is the time of year that it would be nice for all of us who love our pets to be able to bring our pets to church and have you and the other associate pastors bless the animals?" One of my friends had done blessing of the animals often. I knew how he did it. Actually, he did it in the sanctuary. I remember my friend telling about blessing a giant snake as a part of the ceremony.

You see, the problem is I am not a pet person. It is just the way God wired me up, and I don't have pets and am not too impressed with pets. But now I was being asked to hold the animals, to pet the animals, and to get involved. I made some kind of excuses about why I did not think it would work. Then she said, "But if our goal is to make disciples of Jesus Christ, and if God loves his whole creation, including pets, and if pet owners really need to know that God loves their animals, then shouldn't we bless the animals?" I tried to think of an answer, but before I could, she said, "You teach us that we need to do whatever is necessary to lead people to Christ. Maybe this is what would be the very thing that could lead someone like me, who loves her pet so much, to Christ and to his church." As hard as it was for me, we blessed the animals in an appropriate, beautiful ceremony in the fall, and new people have come to Christ because we met that need.

A year or so after the first blessing of the animals, a guy asked me one Sunday, "Do you know why I go to church here?" I knew he was asking that question to trap me in some way, but I answered, "Well, I think so." Then he said, "Oh, no, you don't. I come to church because you prayed for my dog. You see, I never went to church until I came for the blessing of the animals, and because you were so kind and the church was so loving and Christlike, I came back. I am still here."

Oftentimes, the pastor's leadership roles are divided into tasks as administrator, teacher, preacher, worship leader, and counselor. If a church is to grow, the task of being an evangelist must be a priority in the pastor's self job description. Unless the pastor has the passion to reach new people, thinks about it every day, makes it a part of every decision and a priority in terms of time management, it will not work.

Finally, the first place of responsibility for needs-based evangelism is with the pastor. Unless there is enthusiasm and commitment at that level, there will be minimal results.

CHAPTER 16

DECIDE

Our Struggle with Deciding

Change comes out of decision. So much of our paralysis is brought on by the inability to decide. The loss in the church has come because we have decided not to decide. And with apathy or indecision or fear, nothing happens except decline.

Basic for everyone is to make decisions by *group pressure*. We want to keep up with one another. We make decisions by following fads, styles, and cultural influences. It is normal for human beings to want to fit in. The problem in church decision-making that is based on conformity is, so often, the conformity has been to a style of mediocrity or simply maintaining the status quo. Churches today, like all creative institutions that will survive, must make decisions "out of the box." The decisions need to be in response to the culture and responsive to the culture, but not necessarily the way that all the other churches in our denomination or judicatory or neighborhood are doing it. We are called to decide what is Christ's way and what will work in making disciples.

For most organizations caught in the midst of change, conflict, competition, and pressure to get results, we do something even if it's wrong. *Expediency* becomes a decision-making methodology. We decide because we have to decide. Often, under the crisis of expediency or the pressure of finding a solution, we make decisions that are not thought out and not carefully researched and that end in failure. Churches today need to be well-informed, to plan carefully, to make decisions based upon good research, and to be ready to respond to rapid changes with emergency plans and procedures.

Those who study decision-making suggest that some decisions are made by *tradition*— that is, "we've always done it that way." For the church, this concept has oftentimes been the key to our failure. With always doing it the same old way, we've lost our way in the irrelevancy of the same old way. And we come to worship the good old hymns, the good old liturgy, the same old programs without realizing that the people that we're seeking to reach for Jesus don't like the good old music and the good old programs. It's time to decide what traditions should be kept and what should be thrown away, what can be appreciated and revised and rebuilt and what is no longer effective at all and is dysfunctional. The great traditions of faith expressed in the sacraments, in the music, in the liturgies, and in the traditions can be saved. In fact, much of the tradition is of the finest and most effective means to communication today. We just need to sort it out and do what works, not do what is dysfunctional, and quit arguing about it.

Most corporate and institutional decision-making is based upon *goals*—that is, we decide what will accomplish our goals. We set missional purposes and strategies to accomplish those goals. This has become such accepted methodology that we've assumed that it won't work for the church. The truth is that it does work. The decision-making of the church must fit with its goals and purpose.

Our goals, as a church—if they're carefully studied and biblically based—provide an opportunity to direct the life of the church clearly without being caught in the trap of just maintaining what we've always done. If our purpose is clearly to make disciples of Jesus Christ, if we understand we are called to be like the good Samaritan and help need, then our decision will respond to this. We do not need complex rules, regulations, and guidelines if the basic guidelines are Christ-centered and clear.

Deciding the Right

Moses stood before the Hebrew people as they began to go into the promised land. He told them that God's message was that they had a choice. The story recorded in Deuteronomy 29 is a story that is relevant to all of us. Moses said the choice was a blessing on one side or a curse on the other, and we are to choose. Paul, in Galatians 5, describes being either a spiritual person or a nonspiritual person and tells us that the rewards of being a spiritual person are what he calls "fruits of the spirit." Again, the issue is to choose right. Discerning the right is a struggle for the individual and for the church. To choose to follow Jesus and to be a good Samaritan church is a significant choice. We have, in the past, made most of our choices in some form of democratic voting process, and certainly, for many congregations, this is the right way to do it. There are new theories of discernment that offer a way to make decisions with more consensus, but less conflict and less winning and losing as part of the decision-making. The important thing is to discern God's will in a biblically based, prayerful context of a situation in which the grace of God, expressed through Jesus Christ, is the priority, and where we meet the needs of the people who are on the committee or board, as well as seek to meet the needs of the community—that is, being loving should be a part of the whole process from deciding to doing.

There are many congregations across America that are learning better how to make decisions that are respectful for everyone participating in and in harmony with the gospel. Jessica Moffatt, pastor of a growing United Methodist church in the Tulsa area, has helped her congregation make some critical decisions in terms of relocation, redevelopment, and renewal, all based upon careful spiritual discernment. She is a part of a growing number of pastors who have found a discernment process more effective than the old parliamentary procedure.

The Power of the Individual

The problem in decision-making for so many Christians is we are unwilling to take the first step, which is the total commitment of the individual. Without that commitment, we are only a club, another game to attend, a fellowship of shoppers that is always transitional, and a waste of time for so many people. Individual Christians are called to make a decision to make a difference.

The decision-making that is needed today is a radical decision-making during which individual Christians decide that their life counts and they can make a difference. The successful history of the church is a history of those individuals.

It's a story of a pastor who, in undergraduate school, decided that he wanted to accomplish big things for God—to start a church that would become not a struggling shadow of a church, but a church that could make a difference. He chose a denomination in which he saw potential, and Adam Hamilton started twenty years ago what has become the fastest-growing church in Methodism—primarily because Adam decided. William Booth, catching the enthusiastic spirit of the Wesleyan movement, yet being rejected by the leaders of that movement, saw a desperate need for social change in England, and started a new program. The Salvation Army was to provide some of the most significant helping ministry to hurting people around the world. William Booth made the decision and life changed. But the stories are not always stories of people whose names are found in publications of denominations or the history of culture, but ordinary people who make a decision to make a difference.

The pastor of a small, struggling church in a rural community decided to change things around. Her decision and commitment developed a Boy Scout program that was to become the youth program of the community; and the church that was nearly out of business became the principal organization to bring renewal to the young people of that community. Linda Harker was appointed by her bishop to serve a struggling church in a suburban neighborhood. Barely finished with her education, she found herself with the job as a clergywoman struggling against an impossible situation. Linda decided to stay, and she succeeded. She has become the pastor of one of the larger churches pastored by a woman in the United Methodist denomination.

Lou Martin, a devoted Roman Catholic clergy, felt the pressure of his denomination against innovation and new possibilities; and yet, committed with a deep passion for evangelism and a positive understanding of life, he turned his church around and became an example in his part of his denomination of vitality and strength at a time when the denomination was going through hurtful, declining transitions. This success happened only because Lou decided to make the commitment.

In each one of these stories, the key is decision. The laity or clergyperson made the decision that things could change—and they changed. There are, of course, stories of decisions that were made and nothing happened. But when a total commitment is made, something does happen. The success may not always be measured in a way in which others want it measured, but when we commit to God's way—when we give our lives— we save them. For it is true that, as Paul states in Romans, "all things work together for good for those who love God" (8:28). I would challenge the laity and clergy of the church today who read this book to understand that they can make a difference! With all of our limitation and all the ordinary problems, we can make a difference!

In 1990, eight members of my congregation, including myself and my wife, attended a denominational conference in San Francisco. The leaders challenged us to increase our worship attendance to either one thousand by the year 2000 or two thousand by

2000. Our average attendance was six hundred at the time. While still in San Francisco, the team discussed what recommendation we would take back to our congregation. It seemed obvious that the logical solution for the next ten years would be one thousand in attendance, but Stan said no. Stan, a big guy with a big smile and lots of relation skills, simply convinced us that God wanted two thousand rather than one thousand. Even though it seemed impractical and almost stupid, we went along with what Stan believed God wanted us to do. Amazing as it seems, the church bought the recommendation. Our goal became two thousand by 2000.

Christ Church is in a no-growth part of mid-town Tulsa. We don't have new buildings. We did not have adequate parking. The church was a mid- to low-income church. Often, the finances were very bad, and we ran out of money. We had, five years before, gone through a significant old-fashioned church fight. Everything was wrong. No reason to grow. But Stan said we would. He accepted as his slogan, "Each one, reach one." Nothing new about that. Everybody has heard that idea. Church marketing strategy has spoken that slogan over and over, but Stan wouldn't shut up. He taught his Sunday school class about "each one reaching one." Every meeting he went to, he spoke about "each one reaching one." He modeled the standard himself. When he finished teaching his class, he stood in the narthex and greeted people. He volunteered to make calls on all of the visitors. He motivated others to do it; and when others wouldn't do it, he'd do it on his own. By the time Stan died of cancer in the late 1990s, the attendance was more than sixteen hundred. An impossible goal was accomplished. In the story of Christ United Methodist Church in Tulsa, Oklahoma, many things may be given credit for the growth and vitality of the church, but as far as I'm concerned, it's because Stan decided. And when he decided, we all decided. And it worked.

Time to Decide

There are so many decisions for the local church to make. There are so many priorities and issues. It is easy for the church to make its major priority and emphasis on maintaining, rather than on mission or evangelism.

The purpose of this book is to encourage church leaders to place a major priority on reaching new people for Jesus Christ. The methodology to do that is needs-based evangelism. In order for the church to do this, leaders of the church must decide that this is the priority. Leaders of the church must make the decision to place making disciples of Jesus Christ as first, to evaluate every program, activity, and expenditure on the basis of making new disciples of Jesus Christ. Maintenance items are important and must be a part of the priority, but unless the church makes the decision to reach out and grow, it will continue to decline and will no longer have the strength to do the deeds of ministry it has done in the past. If churches do not grow, with the present demographics of the mainline Protestant churches in America, they will simply disappear in the next twenty to thirty-five years.

The decision that must be made by the local church begins *first* with the leaders deciding that God has called them to follow the Great Commission and to make the priority making disciples. *Second*, the decision must be that the local church and its leaders will place the imperative in 1 Corinthians 9:19-23 as their imperative. This is to do whatever is necessary to reach new people for Jesus Christ. *Third*, the decision must be to use meeting needs ministry as a primary means of reaching new people. The *fourth* decision is to analyze where the needs are in the community that the local church has the resources to meet. We cannot do everything, but we can do some things well, and we have the resources to do that. The *fifth* decision is to mobilize the laity to do this ministry. The *sixth* decision is to develop a system of hospitality and relationships that help new people become comfortable within the life of the church as they are reached through the "niche marketing" or needs ministry program of a local church. The *seventh* decision is to place a high priority on being a healthy church, a church in which people can continue to find spiritual growth, blessings, fellowship, joy, and empowerment of worshiping God and celebrating their relationship to his church. The *eighth* is to decide that out of the health of the local church will come more evangelists.

Unless the above decisions are made clearly and maintained, no idea about evangelism, no conversation about the decline, no pressure from denominational executives will make any difference. We will simply ride the slow decline into oblivion.

Some might say that those who do not decide deserve to die. From the author's point of view, for mainline churches, large and small alike, not to decide is a terrible tragedy and a waste of the gifts that God has given us.

The challenge is to decide or die. The reality is to do evangelism or we will die. My prayer is that we will decide that we will do, that we will proclaim, and God's church will grow and new people will become part of the family of God.

CHAPTER 17

THE NEW JERUSALEM

The New Jerusalem

John writes in Revelation 21, "Then I saw a new heaven and a new earth; for the first heaven and the first earth had passed away. . . . And I saw the holy city, the new Jerusalem, coming down out of heaven from God. . . . I heard a loud voice from the throne saying, 'See, the home of God is among mortals. He will dwell with them; they will be his peoples, and God himself will be with them.'" For every person who has committed their life to Christ, for every clergy who has been ordained to the ministry, for every judicatory leader who has accepted the assignment of leadership, this dream must be present. It is the dream that, somehow, the words of the angels at the time of the birth of Jesus will come true: Peace on earth, good will to men.

Oftentimes, our job's only goal is survival from Sunday to Sunday, finishing the sermon before the prelude, raising the budget, pleasing cantankerous church members and insensitive administrators, and simply getting by. But there is inherent in each of us a dream that life can be better and that peace can happen; and there is, in the Christian, a conviction it will happen through the power of our Lord, Jesus Christ.

Modern life is extremely complicated. The present world situation is precarious. Terrorism, nuclear threat, family degeneration, gross depression, uncontrolled secularism, and hedonistic attitude toward life could be the description of our present situation. Yet we believe that human beings can love God, that human beings can show dignity within themselves and love their neighbors. We believe that men and women following God's guidance can change this world and bring the New Jerusalem.

The task of evangelism is not just getting another member in the church, another giver on the roll, another singer in the choir—it is to make the dream come true. It is to do what God said through Jesus Christ. Our goal is not being successful salesmen, our goal is the kingdom of God. Our goal is not winning over the competition, but it is winning the race.

The Addiction of Pessimism

We had finished the monthly denominational meeting. A group of clergy were having lunch together. The conversation was about griping. We were griping about our denominational leaders, our denominational literature, our local churches, our cantankerous laypeople, our salaries, and our society. And then she said it. All she said was, "We had a great Sunday last week." And everyone got quiet. One of her friends said, "What happened, Bethany? Did that old, cantankerous finance chairman finally die?" Everybody laughed. And Bethany said, "No, I mean, really! Attendance was way up, and the worship was fantastic." There was silence, and then someone said, "What happened?" She said, "All the things we had been trying to do—this evangelism program—are working! Really working! I just wanted to tell you it was a great Sunday." It was like someone had poured cold water over everybody. One of the guys said, "You know, I forgot I've got a hospital call I've got to go and take care of." Three more people began to get up from the table, mumbling something about hospitals. In less than three minutes, Bethany was sitting by herself.

We seem to like bad news and don't want to hear about one another's success or success at all. We have become addicted to failure, to hopelessness, and to anger.

The Challenge

Church today needs to begin to celebrate all the good stories! We need to celebrate one another's victories! We need to join one another in leading people to Christ! We need to turn around the pessimism and the lack of hope and optimism and create a new church culture of dreaming, sharing, caring, and helping! Things may change in denominational structures, new churches may be created, new leaders will come to the front, and yet our task will remain—that is, the task of making disciples of Jesus Christ and joining God in his kingdom building. The local church is a basic unit of God's kingdom building.

The purpose of this book is to call for new evangelistic excitement in the local church and to provide a methodology of needs-based evangelism to do that. The goal of the book is for the reader to be motivated, excited, and determined to understand what Paul said in 1 Corinthians 9:23: "I do it all for the sake of the gospel, so that I may share in its blessings." May that excitement be yours.

As it is in many aspects of our lives, there are consequences and clear realities that we can't ignore. In terms of evangelism, if we ignore the need to be evangelistic and to reach new people for Jesus Christ and to build his church, we will decline. If the mainline churches today do not respond to the challenges and possibilities of leading new people to Christ, we will die. The challenge is simply "do or die."

God has given us great opportunities and a methodology taught by Jesus that I have called needs-based evangelism. Needs-based evangelizing is simply doing what the good Samaritan did, what Jesus did, and what we can do. It is an effective way to fulfill the Great Commission.

We must be evangelistic in order to fulfill our responsibilities as the church of Jesus Christ.